inside
golf

dawson taylor

Contemporary Books, Inc.
Chicago

Library of Congress Cataloging in Publication Data

Taylor, Dawson.
  Inside golf.

  Includes index.
  1. Golf. 2. Golf—Psychological aspects. I. Title.
GV965.T2   796.352'3   77-91177
ISBN 0-8092-7804-9
ISBN 0-8092-7803-0 pbk.

All photos courtesy of Jeff Joffe

Copyright © 1978 by Dawson Taylor
All rights reserved.
Published by Contemporary Books, Inc.
180 North Michigan Avenue, Chicago, Illinois 60601
Manufactured in the United States of America
Library of Congress Catalog Card Number: 77-91177
International Standard Book Number: 0-8092-7804-9 (cloth)
                                    0-8092-7803-0 (paper)

Published simultaneously in Canada by
Beaverbooks, Ltd.
150 Lesmill Road
Don Mills, Ontario M3B 2T5
Canada

dedication

To my three golfing companions, my very good friends, Denise Martin, Christine Power, and Dawson Taylor who were privileged to learn their beginning golf from a Master's champion, Horton Smith.

contents

Under the "Rules of Amateur Status" of the United States Golf Association, an amateur forfeits his amateur status by receiving compensation for giving instructions on the golf course, in writing, or in photographs. Although my chances of ever winning the United States Amateur Golf Championship are completely nonexistent, I still would prefer to remain a true "amateur" golfer in the eyes of the U.S.G.A. and in the eyes of my golfing friends. So I should like to state for the record that while my name appears as author of this book, while the writing approach and all of the actual text are mine, the techniques with respect both to instruction and actual play originate primarily in the knowledge, experience, and professional and amateur play of many other golfers whom I have been privileged to know, consult, admire, and imitate during my own lengthy amateur golf career.

I would like to give special credit to the late Horton Smith, professional at the De-troit Golf Club until his untimely death in 1963. Horton lived for golf. He remembered every stroke he had ever taken. He had a reverence for golf, its traditions, and its rules that I feel rubbed off on me and resulted in my own great interest in golf and in my own search for the "how and why" of the effective golf swing.

In my lifetime of reading about golf and observing golf, I have been impressed particularly by the swing techniques of many great golfers as well as the swings of some excellent golfers who perhaps are less than well known to the world. I would like to give credit at this time to many of these golfers, with the realization that even though I name them here, there are countless other stylists of golf who deserve equal credit for one or more of the instructional ideas in this book.

Here they are: Fred Lamb, my first instructor; Al Watrous, great champion of the twenties and thirties and runner-up to Robert T. Jones, Jr., in the British Open of 1926; Robert T. Jones, Jr., whose play I witnessed and whose marvelous books I read avidly; Walter Hagan for his attitude toward winning golf; Ben Hogan; Byron Nelson; Jimmy Demaret; Sam Byrd; Bob Toski; Doug Ford; two extraordinary putters, Deane Berman and Bill Casper; Joe Carr; Marvin Stahl; Arnold Palmer; Jack Nicklaus; Glenn Johnson, five times Michigan Amateur Champion and model in many of the pictures in this book; George Haines; and Gary Wiren.

I also would like to express my appreciation to the United States Golf Association for its many courtesies and especially for its kind permission to quote from the *Rules of Golf.*

I would like to express my sincere appreciation to my "home pro," Michael V. Gallagher, Jr., for his friendship and counsel. My gratitude, too, goes to my "models," Brookes Billman, Mickey Gallagher, Jr., Betty Gallagher, Barbara Romack, Ed Harris, Herb Miller, Al Weller and Jack Van der Molen, as well as to Steve and Odell McDaniel, my prize beginner golfers.

And I thank Little, Brown and Company for their kind permission to quote an excerpt from the book by Tony Lema and Gwilym Brown, *Golfer's Gold.*

introduction

The first thing you may ask is, "Who is this Dawson Taylor who is trying to teach me how to play golf?" You have a perfect right to ask that question. I hope that the answers I supply will encourage you to listen to what I have to say in this book, to read it with enthusiasm, to take to heart some of the ideas in it, and to begin to enjoy the great game of golf as I have enjoyed it for more than forty years of an active business and golfing life.

First, a brief biography. I am the second son of three sons of George M. Taylor, a pioneer automobile dealer in the early 1900s and an avid golfer himself though not a very good one. He was a powerful hitter of the ball but one who rarely scored as low as the 90s. I caddied for my father when I was about eight or nine years old,

and then I didn't want to caddy for him any longer. I wanted my own clubs. When I showed enthusiasm for golf in my early years, my father arranged for me to take golf lessons. A great Scottish professional, Fred Lamb, taught me the fundamentals of golf in a golf net in the basement of the Detroit Athletic Club during the winter. I was eleven years old at that time. My father was a member of Plum Hollow Golf Club in the Detroit district, and there was a "Junior District" Golf Association of the Detroit area. That meant that the sons and daughters of members of the clubs could play in weekly golf tournaments at various golf courses around Detroit.

Although I was a very bad golfer at that time, I entered one of the Junior District golf tournaments along with several other sons and daughters of Plum Hollow club members. I remember well my first tournament at Meadowbrook Golf Club on the outskirts of Detroit. I was small in stature at that time, about four feet, nine or ten inches tall, I believe. The end of that day found me the proud possessor of a $2.50 gift certificate from the J.L. Hudson Company. I was the runner-up in the boy's division of the fifth flight. My score: 127 strokes!

I continued to play Junior District golf for many years and remember the first time I broke the score of 100 . . . with a 97, the first time I broke 90 . . . with an 87, and, finally, the triumph of all, the first time I broke 80 . . . with a 77 at the Detroit Golf Club, which, incidentally, became my "home club" during my adult life.

Needless to say, I was "hooked" on golf at that time and have remained so all my life. By the time I was in college I was playing "70" golf consistently and was captain of the University of Detroit golf team in intercollegiate matches with such fine golf teams as the University of Louisiana, Notre Dame, and Northwestern. I became an avid golf observer. In those days the galleries that attended golf tournaments were not nearly so large as they are today.

After World War II, I entered the automobile business in Detroit with my father and two brothers. For the next 20 years I was a "businessman/golfer" with scores in the mid-70s most of the time. Horton Smith, two-time Master's champion, became my friend and my teacher. Horton was known as one of the finest putters of all time. I worked at incorporating

his putting techniques into my own game and became a very good putter in my own right. I remember in the 1950s having two successive days of 22 putts in 18 holes. I grant you that those figures don't say much for my ability to hit the greens in par figures, but 14 one-putts in any single round is sensational, much less in two rounds in a row. I hold the 9-hole amateur course record at Detroit Golf Club, a 32, with 146 feet of holed putts. I also hold the amateur course record at my present home course, Atlantis Golf Club, a 31 with 6 birdies in the last 7 holes and a total of 96 feet of holed putts. Interestingly, each of these record rounds ended with holing 50- and 40-foot putts for the final birdie.

As you can see, I have been through the golfing mill. I have suffered with a bad slice, a bad hook, shanking, topping—all the woes that golfers are heir to. And even though my game today is the best it has ever been, I am reconciled that I will never be the "scratch" golfer I would like to be. I probably will always make those few mistakes each round that keep me a "three-handicap golfer." But in my personal search for golf perfection, I have found a number of basic things worth repeating. Furthermore, I sincerely believe that I can help you become not only a competent golfer but also a "true golfer"—one who will enjoy one of the greatest sports in the world for the rest of your life.

Great golfers regularly visited the Detroit area to play match and medal tournaments. I had the privilege of scoring for Ben Hogan and Byron Nelson in a match at the Detroit Golf Club in 1941. I watched the diminutive Ben Hogan drive the ball prodigious distances. I saw the smooth rhythmic swing of Sam Snead in his first appearance in the National Open championship held at Oakland Hills in nearby Birmingham, Michigan, in 1937.

Along the way, too, I had instruction from great teachers of the game. More and more my own golf game became standardized. Since the early 1950s I have played at a steady "3 handicap," which means that my average score is about 75 or 76. I have read nearly every book ever written on golf instruction.

I submit these remarks simply as credentials. I have been a beginner and have taught beginners, and I sincerely hope that my experience will benefit your game.

Mickey Gallagher discusses the differences between the swings of taller and shorter golfers with Steve and Odell McDaniel and tells them that sometimes the shorter golfer must use shorter-shafted clubs.

chapter 1

THE BEGINNER

What is a beginner golfer? The dictionary tells us that a beginner is one "who is just starting to learn or to do something." What kind of people are beginners at golf? From experience, I have observed that they fit roughly into three categories. First, there is the young man or woman, sometimes even the child, who becomes interested in playing the game. The desire might spring from the fact that parents or friends are already playing golf and the novice wants to imitate them. Often, the young boy is attracted to the money he can make by caddying and soon discovers that the caddies are permitted to play free on Mondays. He is bitten by the golf bug and starts to play. The girl often starts because her "big brother" plays and the game looks interesting to her.

The second group of beginner golfers seems to consists of adults, young married people or young executives who become successful and want to take up golf for social or business reasons. It is well known that the golf course is an excellent place for closing sales or "making contacts." In this group of golfers you will find the married woman whose husband plays golf avidly. With her children in school a good part of the day (or later in life when her children are married and on their own), that wife suddenly decides that now, for the first time in her marriage, she has the leisure and the inclination to take up golf. This same "married woman syndrome" also may apply to the young wife in the years before she has a family.

As for the third group, in these years of pensions and early retirement, there is a growing interest among older people who never have played golf before but now find themselves with time on their hands and perhaps living near or in a golf community.

In this category, I would like to point out as unusual examples of success at golf during the retirement years Steve and Odell McDaniel, who are good friends of mine and who live at Atlantis in Florida, a golf community. Steve retired from a life-long career on the styling staff of General Motors. At his retirement party, he was surprised to find himself the new owner of a beautiful set of matched woods and irons and a monstrous golf bag. It seems that

Mickey Gallagher explains to Odell McDaniel the differences in weight and length between his standard-size man's driver and her driver, which is specially designed for women's play.

Mickey Gallagher explains to Steve McDaniel the importance of the "trigger" spot in the pad of the right forefinger.

Steve had been saying for years, "Some day, when I retire, I'm going to take up golf." So his friends at GM took him up on the proposition.

Steve and Odell both decided to learn golf when they moved to Atlantis. I wish that I could take the major credit for their ensuing successful careers in golf. But I cannot take any credit other than the fact that I did encourage them to persevere when the going was rough. They both took lessons from golf professional Matt Mattison of the PGA, an outstanding teacher. They played regularly and practiced faithfully. They entered all the club golf events to get even more experience. The result, I am pleased to say, is that both Steve and Odell are most capable golfers. Steve recently posted a score of 87, and Odell now has broken the 100 barrier. Perhaps, even probably, they never will be low-handicap golfers, but, on the other hand, they are golfers of considerable ability, better than a good percentage of players at Atlantis, and, best of all, they are enjoying golf and enjoying their life in retirement. Golf has brought a new and completing dimension to their lives. I am proud of Steve and Odell and hold them up as marvelous examples for beginning golfers to emulate.

So, no matter what personal journey the beginner golfer takes in reaching his or her decision to play golf, once it has been made, and after a few good, solid strokes at the elusive white ball, the golfer is "hooked," usually for life. There is no more avid golfer than the new golfer, no matter what his age may be. He approaches the game with unbounded enthusiasm and always, it seems to me, enjoys golf in a way seldom seen in the golfer who has been playing all his life and is reconciled to his often dull golfing plateau, having no compelling desire for further technical improvement.

The process of learning golf is a slow one. There may be many periods of discouragement. There are various plateaus of achievement, and sometimes it seems to the beginner that the ultimate in his search for perfection in his swing has been reached. The "100 golfer" reaches the 90s and stays there for what he feels is an endless time. The "80 golfer" rarely breaks into the 70s and sometimes even slips back into the 90s.

It is true, too, that all of us vary in our natural athletic ability. Some of us have natural rhythm in our bodies. Others do not. Some people can dedicate themselves to the perfection of their games through long hours of practice. Others do not have the same amount of desire, energy, or determination. Obviously, motivations differ. The urge to excel differs greatly from person to person. Based upon my personal pleasure and satisfaction gained from playing golf for more than forty years, I can state with considerable authority that if you, the ordinary or even extraordinary beginner golfer, will accept the challenge of learning the fundamentals of golf, of applying them regularly in practice and in official play, you will be rewarded with many physical and psychological benefits and will derive great pleasure and personal satisfaction from the development of a sound golf game.

(Left) Mickey Gallagher is teaching his son, Mickey, Jr., who is just beginning to play golf. He is nine years old and a little under five feet tall. He has a driver that is about eight inches shorter than the regular length, with a lighter clubhead and shaft.

(Below, left) Mickey Gallagher is showing Mickey, Jr., how straight he wants to see his left arm at the top of the backswing. Young players are able to build good swings at this time of their lives, swings that will never desert them even if they do not play golf for years.

(Below, right) Mickey is showing Mickey, Jr., that his grip could be improved by sliding that right forefinger farther down the shaft. Young players love to "hit the ball a mile" and should be encouraged to do so even if they don't hit it very straight at times. How to achieve direction can be learned later.

Women golfers often prefer to take instruction from a member of their own sex. Here, Barbara Romack *(on the left)* is shown explaining the fundamentals of the golf swing to her pupil, Betty Gallagher.

chapter 2
YOUR PROFESSIONAL TEACHER

This book is intended to give you, the beginner, a "preview of coming attractions" to the wonderful world of golf and to explain a few fundamental theories and facts about the game, its etiquette and rules, so that you will be encouraged to take it up seriously, learn it well, and, in time, achieve a certain level of proficiency.

From my early days of instruction under the great Scottish professional teachers, Fred Lamb, Davey Millar, and Alex Ross, to the present, with home professional Mickey Gallagher, I have been an avid student of golf, always consulting professional teachers as I encountered various minor problems with my golf swing. I recommend strongly that if you have not been taught by a professional teacher thus far, you seriously consider arranging to do so. Furthermore, I have some advice on the kind of teacher you should select.

You will find, as I did, that every teacher of golf is different from every other. There are "talkers," who will talk the theory of golf to you, and there are "doers," professionals who will watch you swing a few times and then suggest a minor change that may work miracles for you. On the other hand, there are teachers who immediately want to make over your entire swing. You need to find a golf teacher who understands you, your personality, your character, and your attitude toward the game of golf.

Many golf teachers have been accused of making so many and such radical changes in their pupils' games that the result has been, in their own words, "I couldn't hit a ball at all afterward." While this situation may be authentic in some isolated cases, I would like to give you an example from my personal experience that will show the other side of that coin.

In the mid-1950s I found my game in a 78 to 82 rut. I grant you that many players would be pleased to be in a rut such as that, but I was not. I felt that I could truly be a low 70s player. I was determined to improve my game. I went to Horton Smith, the charming and famous (two-time winner of the Master's tournament, in 1936 and 1938) pro, and after telling him I was dissatisfied with my game, asked him if he thought he could improve it.

He knew my game well from long observation. His answer was, "If you are prepared to work at it, I can make you a low 70s golfer. But, I warn you, you may score in the high 80s or even low 90s for awhile!" I accepted the challenge and began a series of lessons with Horton. My swing at that time was long and "wristy." There was a lack of compactness in my swing. Believing that since I was on the short side physically, I had to compensate with a long swing, the backswing of my club often reached well beyond my left shoulder, sometimes even touched my back.

Horton recommended that I make my swing more compact. He shortened my backswing. You can see in a photo on page 41 the point at which I now stop the backward motion of my driver. Other clubs are stopped even sooner. The result of this radical change in my game was just as Horton predicted, scores in the high 80s and a few in the 90s. It took me months of practice and "thinking" to end my bad habit of the loose and long windup. But the results were also exactly as he predicted—at last, scores in the low 70s. Not only did I score in the low 70s in the 1950s but to this day I frequently score in the same range. I even have had the great thrill of scoring in the 60s when everything "went right" and all the putts went into the hole.

So, using myself as an example, I say, "Trust your professional teacher with your game!" Find a teacher that you like and confide in him. Tell him about your bad shots. Don't be impatient and demand instant results. Many of us have muscles that have moved in certain ways all our lives until the day they are told by a golf teacher that they must move a little differently for a proper golf swing. It takes time to change the habits of a lifetime.

You will find, as I did, that you will "fall in love with your grip." For some strange reason, all of us seem to think that the first way we have learned to grip a golf club is the best and only way for us. The slightest change of the thumb farther down the shaft or rotation of either hand in a more or less clockwise direction finds us "fighting the change" and adamantly sneaking back to our first and "best" grip.

This is a most serious problem, in my opinion. But if you understand and accept my "solution," it will add greatly to your enjoyment of golf. As a first step, let me remind you to perform the exercises suggested to build your left side, which will make your left hand and left arm stronger and stronger. Therefore, it will take more and more power in your right hand to take over and pass, or overcome, your left hand and left side as you swing through the ball.

Now doesn't it make sense that if you constantly are gaining more strength in your left hand, the right hand will be able to apply more and more power at impact without overturning the left? It is true, and the conclusion is the "solution" I mentioned above: you must be prepared to change your grip, making the left hand weaker and the right hand stronger as you proceed with your golf career.

Here's another tip about choosing your golf teacher. Do not be surprised if you go from one instructor to another. Your first instructor might prove to be ideal for you, and you might never think of changing. On the other hand, you might find that another teacher will give you an entirely different slant or approach to your individual game, one that solves your golf problems. If so, by all means stick with him or her as you progress in golf. But don't be afraid to change teachers.

I believe strongly that we should seek out those teachers of golf whose physical size and attributes are close to our own. I do not think it makes sense for a small player to go to a tall, strong teacher for instruction or, on the other hand, for a tall, strong player to seek counsel from a small, slight professional teacher. Since I was on the slight side and weighed 117 pounds, standing 5 feet, 7 inches during college golf, I always have made it my habit to observe and study the game of the fine players who most closely match my own stature and shape.

Observe the great professional golfers in action. Nearly every section of the country is visited regularly these days by the Professional Golfers Tour. When there is an announcement of a coming PGA tour event near you, make every possible effort to attend. Be sure to go early enough to watch the players warming up on the practice tee.

When you go to a PGA tour event, go as a student with the intention of getting your money's worth in instruction from these great players. Many of the instructional ideas I have put into this book have come as a result of observing great players, adopting their ideas, and perfecting their techniques in my own game.

Let me give you several examples of these observations and tell you how they affected my golf swing and how they will affect your golf swing, too, if you will let them. Gary Player, the great South African golfer and champion, is perhaps an inch taller than I am and much lighter in weight, yet he has always been able to hit the ball prodigious distances with great accuracy. Therefore, early in my career of golf observation, I made it a point to get to golf tournaments early and watch Gary Player on the practice tee and in practice rounds. You should be aware of the fact that the PGA tour events always allow time for a practice round or two before official play begins, usually on a Thursday so that play will end on Sunday in front of the television cameras.

So I would plan to go to the tournaments a day early and watch, at reduced admission rates usually, the practice in general and the practice round of Gary

Player in particular. I noted several things about his swing that attracted me. First, it seemed to me that his entire swing routine from lining up his shot right on through to placing his feet in the swing—his grip, his rhythm, the length of his backswing, everything—was exactly the same time after time after time. I resolved to imitate him and standardize my own swing. Where in the past I had been stopping my backswing at various points, that is, one time with my club parallel to the ground, another time beyond parallel, another time short of parallel, I resolved to find the *best* spot to stop my backswing and, by avid practice, to perfect my swing so that I could stop every time at exactly that point.

This resulted in my making a short, heavy practice grip and club, which I used for years in the privacy of my bedroom, taking it back 50 to 100 times in a row before a mirror, trying to achieve an exact repetition of backswings to a precise position of body, arms, and hands.

I noted, too, that Gary had a slightly turned-in right knee that he seemed to "kick" toward the ball as he began his swing. This, too, I adopted without really knowing why he made that move. Later, I found out from other analysts of the swing that this practice, this knee move, is an excellent way to keep the body weight on the left side at the start of the swing and to prevent lateral sway of the hips. It forces a proper turn of the hips rather than a slide or sway away from the ball.

On another occasion I watched Gary Player hit 25 pitch shots to a target about 75 yards away and saw that not *once* did he raise his head as he completed his swing. I reasoned that if this sort of practice was good for Gary Player, it would be good for me. I assure you it was good practice for me and will be for you, too, if you try it.

Another time and at another tournament, I watched the great amateur champions Frank Stranahan and Marvin "Bud"

Ward in a crucial early match at Detroit Country Club in the National Amateur championship of 1962. Incidentally, this was the tournament Arnold Palmer eventually won and then made his momentous decision to turn "pro."

I admired Stranahan's game very much. He, too, was no taller than I and yet got amazing distance in his shots. He was well known for his barbells and golf exercises to increase his strength. But what I saw in Frank Stranahan was this. As he walked down the fairway, he would stop and go through imaginary swings without a club in his hands. What he seemed to be doing was imprinting on his mind the importance of a quick lower body move that would then bring the arms and hands through the ball. He would put his hands back in a mock backswing and then whip his lower body down and through an imaginary ball.

I adopted this practice, too, and found that it is an important key to understanding the physical reactions of the golf swing. You will see it reflected in my discussion of the downswing. I thank Frank Stranahan for explaining this concept to me so many years ago, and without a word passing between us.

If you are a woman, in my opinion, you should attempt to get instruction from one of the excellent teachers who is a member of the Ladies' Professional Golf Association. I believe that a woman golfer is more at ease with a member of her own sex as a teacher. For some strange reason, every beginner at golf feels a terrible embarrassment at hitting a bad golf shot. The beginner dreads getting up on a first tee "before all those people" and "making a fool of himself." I assure you that very few golf observers really care how badly or how well you play the game of golf. Most observers and players really are interested in just one thing in other players' games: that they get on with the game with alacrity and don't waste time between shots selecting clubs or practicing their swings.

So, ladies, find that compatible woman professional who will teach you the game. She will know more about the proper club weight and swing-weight for your physical size and shape. She will have the sympathy and understanding that may be lacking in a male teacher. And, furthermore, a "lady doctor" of golf may lessen your embarrassment at a bad shot and add to your overall enjoyment of the game.

It is estimated that there are more than nine million women golfers in the United States today. At first, in the early 1900s when women began to play the game seriously, they were forced to use clubs designed for the size and strength of the male player. But now golf equipment manufacturers are very much aware of the tremendous woman golfer's market and supply beautifully made golf clubs especially suited for women.

There is no doubt that the average woman has less finger, hand, arm, and body strength than her counterpart male player. Therefore, the woman player should use lighter clubs than the male golfer, and if she is shorter in height, she should use clubs with shorter shafts as well. Golf courses have "ladies' tees" that shorten each hole by 20 to 75 yards. This is only proper because the woman golfer's game is, as a rule, not long enough or strong enough to master the length of a golf course designed for the male player. The woman golfer must adapt her game to her physical strength and ability to strike the golf ball. Where the male golfer may be swinging a 2-iron that will propel the golf ball 200 yards, the woman player may find that her longest club, the driver, will only give her 175 to 180 yards off the tee.

Fortunately, we have witnessed the rise of the Ladies' Professional Golf Association during the last 25 years. Today, in nearly all localities of the country there

Mickey Gallagher, member of the PGA, points out to Brookes Billman that his wrist position might be a little flatter in order to give him more power and to prevent a hook. Notice that Brookes uses an interlocking grip. He says that is the most natural-feeling for him because he has short fingers.

are many competent women instructors in golf. Here pictured, Barbara Romack, a member of the Ladies' Professional Golf Association, is teaching Betty Gallagher of Atlantis Golf Club, Florida. Barbara was the United States women's amateur golf champion in 1954 and was the runner-up for the same title again in 1958. She was a member of the Curtis Cup teams that represented the United States in international women's golf against Great Britain and Ireland in 1954, 1956, and 1958, before she turned professional. Barbara is an outstanding example of the success that women professionals have in teaching other women to play golf. She herself is not very tall and is slightly built yet strikes the ball considerable distances with a smooth, rhythmic swing. Several of her pupils have compiled excellent golf records as a result of her expert tutelage.

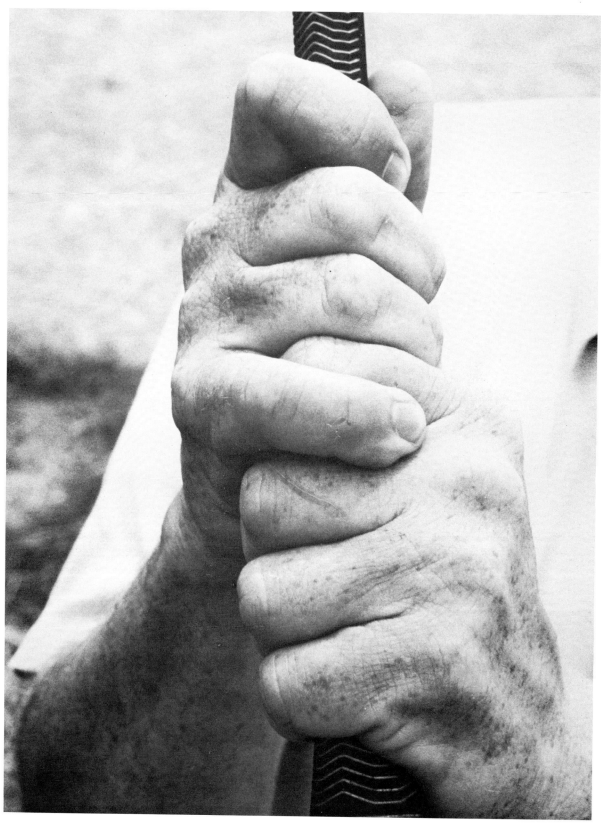

Here is a view of the customary overlapping grip (Vardon grip), which probably is used by 90 percent of all golfers. It is meant to give equal balance to the pressure of each hand on the club and to allow them to act as a unit in the swing. Note that the little finger of the right hand fits into the slot between the forefinger and second finger of the left hand.

chapter 3

THE GOLF SWING AND GRIPS

Consider the golf swing that you are going to build for yourself a huge jigsaw puzzle. A jigsaw puzzle, as we both know, is not complete until the last piece has been inserted into the overall picture. The same principle applies to the golf swing. It has many separate pieces; yet when all of its parts are put together properly, the result is a smooth, rhythmic, and effective golf swing.

We will focus on the individual parts of the golf swing one by one, but do not conclude that the swing is a disjointed hodge-podge. It is not. An automobile engine is made of many working parts, but when they are all put together, they work to produce a single result. We can observe what the piston rod is doing in a functioning engine without losing sight of the fact that it is merely an important, vital part of the complete engine.

Here are the parts of the golf swing that we will examine one by one in future chapters. When they are understood and put together intelligently, they result in an efficient, compact, and repeating golf swing. The various ways the golf club can be gripped will be discussed in this chapter.

The shoulder "tilt," or swing plane
The steady head
The ball position at address
The "one-piece" takeaway
The stances—square, open, and closed
The straight left arm
Rhythm and balance in the golf swing
The top of the backswing
The "stop" at the top of the backswing
The start-down from the top of the swing;
    the left side "pull-down"
The release through the ball
Standing tall at the finish

11

THE GRIP

There has been a great deal of discussion and even controversy for many years over the "proper" way to grip the golf club. You will hear golfers talk about the "Vardon grip," the overlapping grip, the baseball grip, and about strong and weak positions of the hands. You should understand the basic elements of all of these grips so that you can make your personal decision as to how you can most effectively grip and swing the golf club.

There is no doubt but that the first golfers held a golf club with both hands in the same way an ordinary person would grip an axe—hands separated from each other but as close together as possible. It was obvious that the closer the hands, the more the "hit" at the golf ball was a single, undivided effort, that is, one in which neither hand was more in control than the other at the moment of striking.

Then, in the early days of golf, Harry Vardon, a great golf champion, adopted a grip that J.H. Taylor, another fine golfer of the early days, had experimented with and found more practical than the separate hands style. The idea was that by overlapping the little finger of the right hand, considerably more compactness of grip was obtained. The little finger could be on top of the left forefinger, or, as the grip developed among other players, the little finger could slide into the slot between the first and second fingers of the left hand. (See photo.)

The "new style of grip," called the "Vardon grip" after the master golfer who popularized it, was widely adopted by the golfers of that day. Today, the Vardon

This is a version of the overlapping grip that places the little finger of the right hand on top of the forefinger of the left hand rather than in the slot between the forefinger and second finger of the left hand. It is a good grip but not as "solid" as the Vardon version.

The interlocking grip is often used by players who have small hands. Note the interlocking of the left hand forefinger with the little finger of the right hand. Since Jack Nicklaus uses this grip with great success, many players of the modern era are also adopting it for their games.

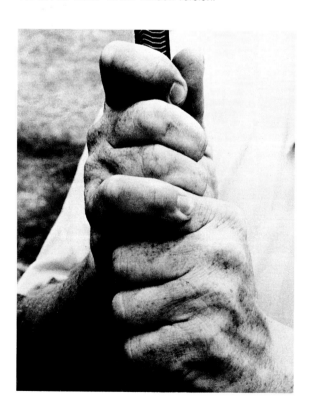

This is the "baseball," five-finger," or "two-handed" grip used successfully by professionals Bob Rosburg and Art Wall, among others. The left thumb may be enclosed inside the grip of the right hand for another variation of this grip. There is definitely a less unifying effect with the baseball grip, as each hand has more of a tendency to act independently of the other.

style of overlapping grip probably is used by 90 percent of the golfers of the world.

But there are exceptions, and notable ones at that. Jack Nicklaus uses the interlocking grip, Bob Rosburg uses the baseball grip. And there are other excellent golfers who, for one reason or another, have found that they need to grip the club in what could be considered unorthodox ways in order to swing it most effectively.

Let's consider the baseball grip first. It is just what it purports to be, a grip with right hand below the left on the golf club and no interconnection between the hands, as in the Vardon grip with its connecting little finger and forefinger. Some golfers with small hands find that this grip is more satisfactory than any other.

The interlocking grip is one in which the little finger of the right hand is "interlocked" by placing it through the opening between the first and second fingers of the left hand, all the way down to the web between the two fingers. This is a compact grip, you will find, and one that is probably second in general use among golfers of the world.

I suggest that you experiment with all of these grips before you decide upon the one that you will use most of the time. My tutor was Horton Smith, two-time Master's champion, and I remember well that he would change occasionally from the overlapping grip to an interlocking grip and would stay with it for a month or two. He would say, "It gives me a new perspective on the problem of gripping the club so that the hands work as a unit. It helps me to understand what the beginner golfer goes through in trying to decide how he should grip the club."

As you will see from the illustration that shows the grip open, the left thumb usually is put down the shaft and enclosed within the grip by folding the right hand

Here is a view of the left hand alone on the shaft in what is called a moderately strong position. Many golfers find that they get the best results from their grips when the "V" of this hand points to the right shoulder. Remember that the last three fingers are the most important. They must be kept tightly clenched in order to resist the torque that will be imparted to the clubhead at impact. Note, too, that this grip has what is called the short thumb position.

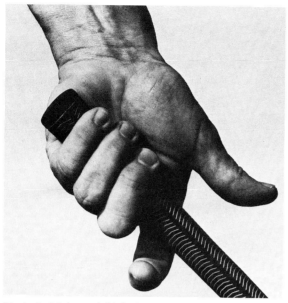 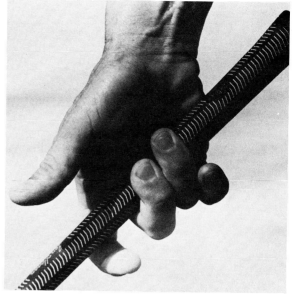

Illustrated *(above. left)* is the position of the last three fingers of the left hand. They are truly the most important of all the fingers in the grip because they provide the foundation for it. If they let go during the swing. the swing usually fails. I cannot emphasize too strongly the absolute necessity for you to build strength in these fingers of your left hand and to remain constantly aware of their tension on the shaft of the club as you swing. Note, too, the way the butt of the shaft rides against the fleshy pad at the heel of the hand. *(Above, right),* the third and fourth fingers of the right hand along with the trigger spot in the right forefinger are the strongest pressure points in the right-hand part of the grip. Grip them very tightly around the club shaft. They are important for the power of the right-hand hit.

over it. This is not necessarily true all the time. Some golfers who use the interlocking grip prefer to lessen strain on the thumb in the backswing and will allow the left thumb to come through and under the right hand. This variation gives less compactness to the grip, in my opinion, but perhaps you will find it satisfactory for your own use.

Now that we have discussed golf grips in general, let us dissect the grip more completely. The final goal is to choose your own grip, one that will give you the most efficient swing, one that repeats time after time and sends the golf ball straight on its way in the direction you want it to go.

Basically, the two hands are opposed to each other on the golf club but opposed to each other in such a way that neither hand overpowers the other. You want the two hands to work together as a unit. For example, take a golf club in hand, separate your two hands by about two inches, and attempt to strike the golf ball. It will be ob-

vious to you that there is an instability, that neither hand is "working" with the other in the final strike of the golf ball. It is this separateness of the hands that must be eliminated in the golf grip. Strive for compactness and unity.

It is most important that you find the grip style that gives you this unity. I suggest that you try the Vardon grip first, and then if it does not work, experiment with the interlocking. When you have settled on the right grip, you are well on your way to building a successful golf swing.

THE "LONG THUMB" VERSUS THE "SHORT THUMB"

There is a difference of opinion among golf instructors as to the position of the left thumb on the golf shaft. (See the photos.) A great deal has to do with the anatomy of the hand, of course. That is, the person with a long thumb must necessarily extend it down the shaft farther than the person with a short thumb. But everyone will find that there are really two positions for the left thumb in his grip, one with the thumb squeezed as close as possible to the side of the left forefinger, and the other with that same space a little more open and the thumb extending down the shaft, away from the golfer.

You yourself will have to find which position is the best for you, the most comfortable, the most efficient, the one that gives you the best control over the golf club at all times in your swing. Notice that if you extend your thumb into the "long thumb" position, your backswing is considerably

The left-hand grip using the "long thumb." You will find that this style of grip will enable you to control the length of your backswing because there will be pressure on the thumb at the top. There is a middle ground, too, between the long and the short thumb, and many golfers use it to get the advantages of each. Try both styles and decide for yourself.

The "short thumb." While a big factor is the length of your thumb, you will find that you can slide it down the shaft in your grip or hold it up tight to the left forefinger. The short thumb position permits a fuller swing. You will have to experiment and find the best position for your left thumb on the shaft.

more controllable at the top. This is most desirable. However, you may also find that there is strain on the thumb, too, and possibly pain in the stretched muscles at the root of the thumb. You may have to com- promise with an in between position for your thumb. The important point is that once you have decided to stay with the short thumb or with the long thumb, you must use that grip consistently. If you don't, you will introduce a variable into your swing that will prevent you from at- taining the consistent result that you de- sire. This is not to say that you never should change your thumb position or, for that matter, any other part of your grip. But make changes only after solid think- ing about the situation and an understand- ing of what you are doing.

An example of the so-called "weak position" for the left hand in the grip. Note the "short thumb" position as well. This grip is an anti-hooking grip for persons who are apt to throw the right hand into the shot and let the wrists roll over at impact.

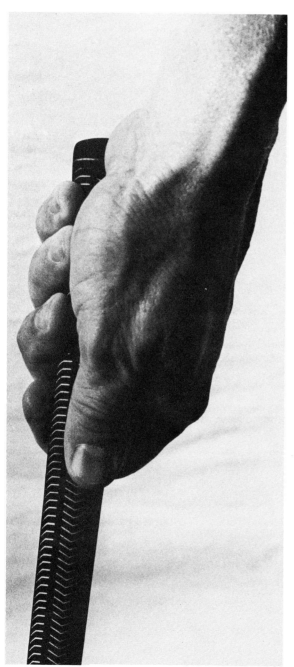

A very "strong" grip. The "V" made by the left thumb and left hand is pointing well to the golfer's right, as is the "V" of the right hand and right forefinger. Both hands are said to be in "strong" position. There is more of a tendency to hook the ball with a grip such as this and for the right hand to roll counterclockwise at impact as the left wrist breaks down, allowing the roll of the wrists to occur. Many good golfers use this grip be- cause it is a powerful one, but for success they do not allow the right hand to turn over at impact or "pass the left hand" until the ball is well on its way to the target. Arnold Palmer uses this grip, and you may recall the distinctive way in which he forces his club to follow the ball on its way to the target, never letting his left wrist break down.

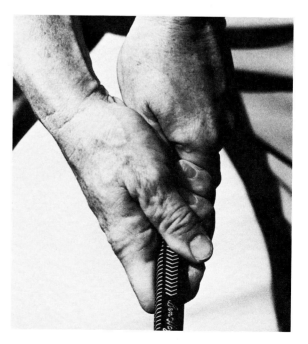

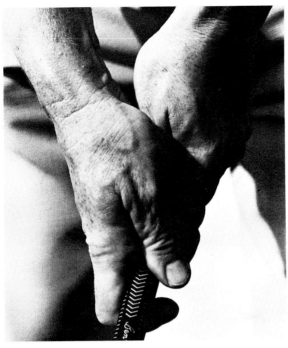

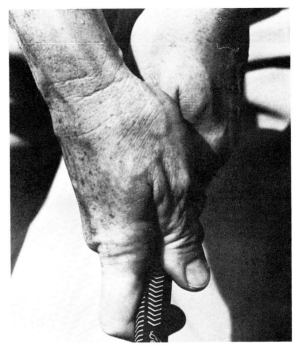

Here is a grip that is said to be much "weaker" than the grip shown in the previous illustration. Note how the right hand has been moved in a clockwise fashion and now is considerably more on top of the shaft. The left hand, too, has been moved in clockwise fashion and now is pointing to the golfer's head, not to his right shoulder. This is the grip for a strong right-handed person who is inclined to hook the ball, as it places the right hand in a position where it is less apt to turn over at impact.

This example of a strong grip is not as strong as the one shown on the opposite page. The "V"s of both hands point upward to the right shoulder. Notice the bulge in the pad of the forefinger of the right hand. It indicates the pressure being exerted there against the club. This is the trigger spot in the grip, which allows the right hand to hit through the ball with great force without overcoming the resistance of the left.

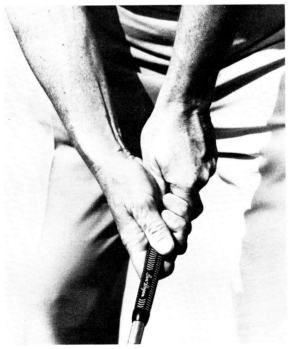

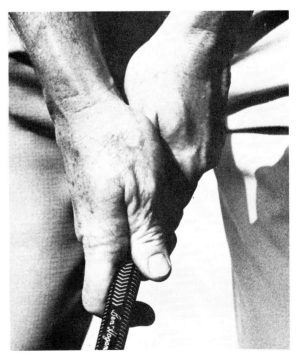

Here are two close-up views of the golf grip properly assembled. Note the differences between them. The grip on the left is said to show "strong" positions in both right and left hands. The grip on the right is said to show a "weak" grip, in that each hand is turned in a more counterclockwise position so that the "V"s of the thumb and forefinger now point to an area inside of the golfer's right shoulder. This "weak" grip is the one that should be used by the golfer with predominant right-hand strength. The "strong" grip, on the other hand, is the one especially suited for the golfer with less right-hand strength. Remember, too, that you might find it useful to use a combination of these two styles, that is, put your left hand in "strong" position and your right hand in "weak" position. Experiment and find your own best working grip!

Mickey Gallagher and Brookes Billman illustrating their shoulder planes. Note that Mickey, being taller than Brookes, has a more tilted plane and clears his jaw nicely as he takes his backswing. Brookes, on the other hand, has a lesser tilt, a flatter swing, and difficulty clearing his chin in his backswing. It is possible that if Brookes adopted a greater angle of tilt, he might be able to swing more effectively. Each golfer must find his own most suitable, or *workable*, shoulder plane.

chapter 4
THE SHOULDER TILT

In a sound golf swing the golfer takes the golf club away from the ball with his hands, arms, and, in effect, with his entire body. He continues to bring the club back until he reaches a point anywhere from shoulder height to above his head, at which point the backswing of the club ends and the swing reverses itself. The golfer then is said to be in his downswing toward the ball.

We will discuss some of the mechanics of the swing later. For now, I want you to consider carefully the "backswing-downswing" sequence. There are three distinct ways to get this job done. The first and most approved for a sound golf swing is to swing the club back and upward and then down and forward in exactly the same path, or "plane." The second way is to take the club back and upward and then down and forward from an inside position (see photo), and the third way is to proceed down and forward from an outside position (see photo).

Try to achieve a swing plane that stays the same both in backswing and in downswing, and avoid building a swing that uses a different plane, whether "outside-in" or "inside-out," for the downswing.

Now, what about the angle of that swing plane? Once more, I want you to look carefully at the photos of Mickey Gallagher and Brooks Billman in which they are demonstrating different angles of swing plane. I call this phase of the game the "shoulder tilt." Perhaps if you think of it that way, it may be clearer than thinking of a "shoulder plane." When the shoulders are tilted toward the ball at a certain angle that allows them to clear the chin readily in the backswing, the correct shoulder tilt has been achieved.

You will have to find your own angle, or tilt. I am five feet, seven inches in height. I am of stocky build, as you can see from the photographs. My neck may be a half-inch or one inch shorter than that of a thin American male of the same height. My arms are short, too, being only thirty-two inches long, whereas most men my height have arms two to four inches longer. All of these physical characteristics and figures add up to the fact that, taking into consideration my height, my general body shape, and my head and neck configuration, a swing plane/shoulder tilt of about forty degrees from the horizontal is the most effective one for me to use for my repeating golf swing.

In order to find your own most effective swing plane, you must realize that there are several fundamentals to observe. The first, an absolute necessity, is that you are able to move your left shoulder under your chin and clear your chin without forcing it to move. Your chin must remain in the steady position we have already discussed. The head is not lowered but, rather, held so that the chin juts out. This jutting out allows better clearance of the shoulder under the chin.

The second necessity in finding your proper shoulder tilt is the realization that you must squat, or "sit down to the ball," during your swing. See the photos for examples of proper and improper sitting down to the ball. Of course, this can be exaggerated to a point where an efficient swing cannot be developed. But I leave it to you to understand these two necessities for determining the correct swing plane, or shoulder tilt, for yourself.

Many golfers turn their heads slightly away from the ball as they start into their

Steve McDaniel is being advised by Mickey Gallagher that he must get more shoulder tilt at the ball so that his left shoulder can pass more easily under his chin. Notice that Steve has broken his left elbow in his backswing. While this is normally considered a swing fault, it is one that Steve manages to compensate for satisfactorily in his downswing.

backswing. Jack Nicklaus is an outstanding example of this trait. The purpose is to allow a fuller backswing, to clear the chin with the left shoulder as we have discussed. Jack gets his head back to the steady, original position as soon as he begins his downswing, and it remains "behind the ball" as he lets his right shoulder take his head up as he proceeds through the ball and into his follow through.

This is the shoulder plane, or tilt, that I have found effective for my five-foot-seven-inch height and the length of my arms. It is the angle at which I can comfortably get my left shoulder under my chin in my backswing. Each golfer must find this angle for himself.

Below is another example of incorrect shoulder plane. In this case, by holding my hands too low I have forced my shoulders into a plane that will not allow a proper swing. The result would be a cramped swing, and because the clubhead is necessarily held so low, it is probable that the heel of the club would strike the ground first and cause inaccuracy. Note that my proper swing plane is somewhere between two extremes.

This shoulder plane or tilt is too flat. If I were to swing from this position, my left shoulder would not clear my chin. The proper shoulder plane must provide a satisfactory method for allowing the upper body to turn under the head, which is held steady. If this plane is too flat, the turn cannot be accomplished.

Here and on page 24 are two separate views of what you should see in the few seconds after you have completed a successful swing. Your head should have remained in a tilted position in relation to the horizon. If your swing is on the "flat" side, you will see the objects on your horizon tilted at about a 15° to 20° angle. If you have a more upright stance and swing, the angle will be less, probably in the range of 35° to 45°. Remember, if you do not see this view after your shot, you have swung improperly and probably have straightened up your body too soon instead of remaining down with a steady head.

chapter 5

THE STEADY HEAD

One of the most common expressions in golf is, "You missed that shot because you didn't keep your head down!" And, in alibiing for a missed shot, you will hear many a golfer say, "I looked up!"

In my opinion, and I am certain that many other teachers of golf will agree with me, "keep your head down" is bad advice for the beginner golfer as well as for advanced players. The advice should be to keep your head *steady* as you make your swing, and then as you swing through the ball, let your head turn and rise with the natural movement of your right shoulder under your chin. Examine carefully the accompanying illustrations that show what the golfer should see in the fractions of seconds immediately after he has struck the ball. Notice that the horizon is tipped about 45 degrees in one photo and about 20 degrees from the horizontal in the other. When the golfer has this "tipped view" of

his shot as it wings toward the target, he knows that most likely he has made a good swing at the ball. On the other hand, if the golfer sees the trajectory of his shot at a 90 degree angle to the horizon, he may presume that he did not make a good swing.

The golfer's head is the center of the axis around which the golf swing is made. If you picture a door on hinges opening and closing against a door jamb, always striking the striker-plate at the door latch in exactly the same place, you will have a concept of the steadiness and the repetitiveness you are seeking.

I cannot overemphasize the importance of the golfer's steady head. Like the hinge on a door, it cannot and must not move from its center point of the swing or else the golf club will not return to its proper place in the swing, directly behind the golf ball, ready to send it properly on its way. While there are exceptions to this state-

ment, and we will discuss such variances later when we talk about the "individual swing," accept for now that the most important fundamental in the golf swing is the steady head.

There are several dimensions in which the head may not remain steady. First, it may move to the right along the swing plane. Second, it may move up or down, farther away from the ground or closer to the ground. Third, it may move forward or backward. Besides, there may be combinations of these movements, such as down and backward, for instance. Any head movement that is not steady (notice that I say "steady," not rigid or unmoving) will necessitate a compensatory reverse movement in order to get the head back to its original striking position.

Let me digress at this point to tell you an anecdote about Paul Harney, an excellent player for many years. In the 1950s I saw Paul play in a Professional Golfers Association championship at Plum Hol-

low Golf Club near Detroit. Paul was known to be a very long driver. I wanted to see how he did it. I watched him and was amazed to see that as he took his backswing, his head moved to the right a good three or four inches. However, as Paul came through the ball, he moved his head back to its original position. Obviously, he was successfully compensating for the movement of his head. I did not see Paul swing again until a few years ago in another PGA tournament. This time I noted that his head was steady and the "bad move" of his head had been eliminated from his swing.

There are other good golfers who move their heads and "get away with it," but they are few. A notable example is the new "star" of the professional golf tour, Ben Crenshaw. He is a head-mover. In my opinion, as he progresses in golf, you will see him eradicate that fault from his swing—or else you will not find Crenshaw on the tour.

Here is an overhead view of Glenn Johnson demonstrating the proper position of
the ball at address. The ball is on a line that runs out from the inside of his left shoe.
Note the closeness with which he holds his elbows, adding to the compactness of
his swing. Note, too, the "cocked" right knee, which puts his weight on the left side
of his body to start. Glenn will start his takeaway with a "kick," or "press" to the left
with that right knee, which will provide him with his one-piece takeaway in the
opposite direction.

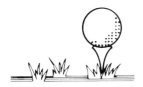

chapter 6

BALL POSITION AT ADDRESS

What are we trying to do when we make a golf swing? Of course, we are trying to drive a golf ball straight at a definite target. Typical targets are the center of the fairway on a long hole, the green, and then the flagstick itself as we near the hole. On every shot in golf the golfer is aiming, or should be aiming, at a target. One of the misconceptions of the beginning golfer is that he need not aim his shot until he nears the green. This is not true. On every shot the golfer must have a target in mind, a target in view. As you will come to understand when you progress in your game, you must perfect a swing that stays "on target" until after the ball has left the face of the club.

As the picture shows, there are several different positions in which the golfer may place his ball in making his swing. A good rule is that you should start out by positioning the ball on a line that runs parallel

from the inside of your left shoe. Probably 90 percent of all golfers use this line and position with success. The reason is that it seems to allow the clubhead to reach its maximum acceleration just before it strikes the ball. Furthermore, it seems to be a comfortable place to put the ball for most golfers.

But, remember, there are another 10 percent who find their best success with the ball positioned either forward of that inner shoe line or behind it. You will find as your game develops that you will want to try "new ideas" in the hope that you can hit the ball harder, straighter, or more consistently. I recommend that you try these variations in placement of the ball later on in your golf career.

As you experiment with placing the ball forward in your stance, more off the toe of your left foot, you will discover that as the ball is moved the least bit forward, it be-

These are the various places the golfer may position his ball at address. The line running from the center of the left shoe is probably the position most often used by golfers, but individual variations may occur, such as off the left toe or well back near the center of the stance. This is a matter of choice for each player. You should start out with the "normal" position, which should give you the best contact and allow your hands to stay on line with the target. After your game has settled down, experiment with the other variations. Your ability to stay with the ball with your hands and arms is of prime importance in the decision.

comes more and more difficult to keep your left wrist from "breaking down" as you hit the ball, more and more difficult to keep the clubhead square to the target line and the clubhead moving down that line as it strikes the ball and the ball comes off the clubface. You may find that a forward position is impossible for you to use because you cannot physically maintain the clubhead on the target line and are forced to bring the clubhead across the line to the left, putting spin on the ball from left to right and, as the expression goes, "developing a wicked slice."

The opposite may prove true as you move the ball backward in your stance, more toward the center of your body. You will find that it becomes more and more difficult for you to get the clubface back to square with the ball as it strikes it. The result may be that with the clubface still open, your shots go to the right. Another

result may be that with the realization that you must get the clubface closed at impact, your right hand desperately tries to force it closed too rapidly, in fact, is still closing (turning from right to left, or counterclockwise) as it strikes the ball. In that event, you either hook the ball with a counterclockwise spin or else "smother" the shot with a "duck hook," which runs immediately to the left of your target line.

Experimenting will show you the best place to position the ball at address. Start with it in the conventional position, off your inner left sole, and work out a swing from there. Later, experiment with the ball position. Trust your professional teacher to analyze your swing and help you find not only the best position of the ball at address but also every other "best position" for you in grip, in stance, at the top of your backswing, and in every other fundamental of the swing.

Glenn Johnson is showing the one-piece takeaway in a move practically straight away from the ball. Note that the clubhead has barely moved inside the line of flight to the target. Note, too, that his hands and wrists are in the same aspect as they were at the address position. The golfer should have the feeling that he is taking the club straight along that line running from the target through the ball, that he is stretching all the muscles in his right side as he makes this move. That sets up the beginning tension of the backswing, tension that will build even more as the shoulders turn against the lower body.

chapter 7

"ONE-PIECE" TAKEAWAY

After proper grip, the next most important segment of the effective golf swing is an effective takeaway. By takeaway we mean the first second or so of the movement of hands, arms, and body as the golf club is "taken away" from behind the golf ball and starts its motion into the backswing.

There are three possible methods of takeaway and infinite variations between these three methods. There is no question that the "one-piece" takeaway is the best and most effective for nearly all golfers. By that expression we mean that the golfer's hands, arms, upper body, and lower body all move at the same time in the motion of taking the club back, away from the ball. There is a feeling of unity, an absence of disjointedness, a feeling that there are unseen rubber bands encircling the arms at about the location of the forearms and elbows, and that everything is moving in syn-

chronization at the same time.

The one-piece takeaway should be done so that the hands, in their progress back in the swing, "stay with the club," wrists unbroken to what might be considered a good distance behind the ball before there is any sign of the eventual wrist break, or wrist "cock," as it is often called. (See photo.) In the one-piece takeaway the hands and wrists remain firm, appearing to be in exactly the same relationship to each other as they were at the address position. (See photo.)

Here is where the first two methods of takeaway begin to differ from each other. The first method allows the hands and wrists to begin their cocking motion when they are 14 to 18 inches away from the ball. The second method, or "all-in-one-piece" takeaway, carries the unbroken wrists and hands even farther into the backswing, sometimes up to shoulder height before the wrist cock is allowed to occur.

The third method of takeaway has a rapid wrist cock that occurs almost immediately as the clubhead braces the ball. This action is called "picking up the club," and while there are some good to great golfers who use this method successfully, it is my recommendation that beginners make every attempt not to do it. Watch Jerry Barber, Miller Barber, even new golf star Hubert Green and you will see this almost instantaneous club "pick up" in their backswings. In spite of it, these golfers manage to coil their bodies properly and execute a timed, successful swing. I do not

Glenn is demonstrating his excellent "one-piece" takeaway. Note that although his club has traveled several feet into his backswing, his hands and wrists remain in the same unbroken position they were in at the start of his swing. His shoulders have begun to turn, and his lower body is beginning to wind up against the resistance of his right leg and right side. His head remains steady over the ball although he has allowed it to turn slightly to the right to facilitate his big shoulder turn.

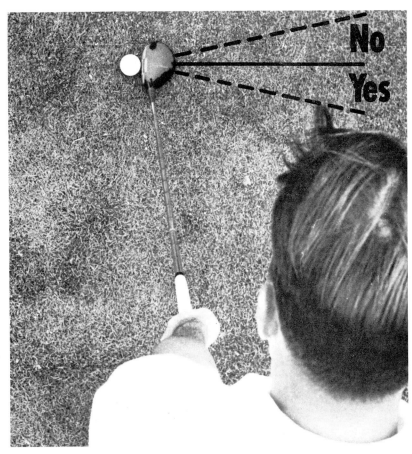

These are the "go" and "no go" takeaway positions. Depending upon the ability of the golfer to take his club straight away from the ball, the takeaway line will be directly away from the ball on the target line or else on the inside of that line, as shown above. A takeaway outside that line in the "No" area of this photograph leads to an ineffective swing from the outside-in and should be avoided.

believe that the beginner golfer can make this quick pick up move and prosper at golf.

To summarize, take the club away as far as you comfortably can in your backswing with unbroken hands and wrists and with arms and body feeling as if they were "all-in-one-piece."

This is the open stance, which is the opposite of the closed stance. This is an exaggeratedly open stance, with the left foot drawn severely away from the line to the target. It often can be seen in use by golfers who have a chronic slice, as it is very difficult to do anything else than slice across the ball at impact, that is, make it spin in clockwise fashion. This stance might be used occasionally by the player who is attempting to slice the ball around some obstruction such as a tree. He might alter his grip to a "weak" position, as well, in order to put the proper spin on the ball.

chapter 8

THE STANCES

Glenn Johnson is demonstrating a swing position in a "square" stance. Both feet are on a line running directly toward the target. Note the straight line running from his left shoulder down his left arm and through the club shaft to the ball. Glenn's right shoulder is lower than his left because his right hand is on the shaft lower than his left. His knees are flexed, and he is "sitting down to the ball." His eyes are directly on the back of the ball, and he is about to "kick off" with his forward press, the move of his right knee toward the ball that starts the entire swing smoothly in its backward motion.

Glenn is demonstrating an inside swing arc here. This style is often the natural result of a closed stance, evident here in the right foot drawn farther away from the line of flight than the left foot. While this type of swing definitely will keep the clubhead inside the line (which, of course, is preferable to having it outside the line), it is conducive to a hook. The golfer who adopts this stance must have extremely good left hand and wrist control so that the right hand does not roll through the shot and produce a right-to-left spin on the ball.

Here Glenn Johnson demonstrates his normal positioning of the club off the inside of his left shoe for his drive. Glenn plays a "square" stance, which means that his feet are both positioned in the line of flight. Note that his toes are turned out, away from the center of his body. That helps him keep his balance and allows a free and easy turn both in the backswing and the forward swing.

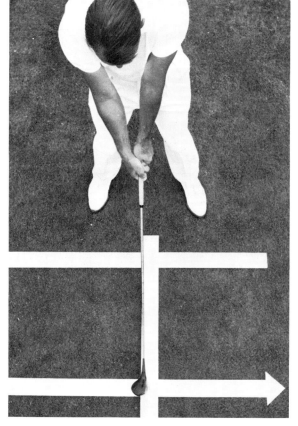

This is an exaggeratedly closed stance to illustrate some of the variations possible in the golf swing. This stance is taken with the right foot drawn away from the line to the target and is used by the player who wishes to move the ball from right to left, "play a hook," as the expression goes. He might also alter his grip to a "strong" position so as to roll the clubface at impact and "work the ball" from right to left with counterclockwise spin.

Mickey Gallagher demonstrates his full swing. Notice his flat wrist, in excellent position, and his right elbow pointing downward, ready to return to his right side the moment he begins his downswing. Notice, too, that his left arm is fairly but not rigidly straight and that his shoulders have turned so that his left shoulder is pointing at the ball.

chapter 9
THE STRAIGHT LEFT ARM

Horton Smith often used this adage about the golf swing: "The function of the left hand and arm is to measure the swing. The function of the right hand and arm is to speed up and 'square up' the golf club-face at impact."

With this thought in mind, consider the role of the left hand and arm in the swing. You have assumed a suitable stance at the ball. Your left hand and arm are extending down from your shoulder to the ball in essentially a straight line from shoulder to grip to clubshaft. You have the feeling that if you did not place your right hand on the club at all, the left hand and arm could take the club away from the ball in a one-hand, one-arm backswing and be able to return the clubface satisfactorily to its original spot behind the golf ball. (See photo.)

The left arm remains "unbroken" in a good golf swing. It is true that in the early days of golf, before a great deal of analysis had been given to the swing, many early champions did "break" their left arms at the top of the backswing and then recover its firmness and straightness on the way back down before hitting the ball.

It is also true that a few good golfers of the modern era break their left arms and "get away with it" with good results. But for the beginner golfer, I strongly recommend that you consider your left arm as practically inflexible during your backswing. You will find, in the long run, that this will pay off in increased accuracy and control in striking the ball.

Let's look at the problem from the physical standpoint. With an unbroken left arm during the swing, your club extends,

39

This demonstration of drawing back the arrow and putting tension on the bow is an attempt to give you a mental picture of the tension that you must develop and must *feel* strongly as you make your golf swing. The greater the controlled tension you build between your hands, arms, and upper body as it is coiled against the resisting lower body muscles of the left leg, left side, and left shoulder, the more power you will be able to develop and the more distance you will be able to drive the ball.

let us say, 34 inches down from the shoulder, down the shaft past an extended, straight elbow, to the ball some 42 inches away. The second that you allow any breaking of the left elbow, you are shortening your club by a half-inch, possibly an inch or more, depending upon the extent to which the left elbow is broken.

The same things we observed about the moving head vs. the steady head apply to the broken vs. the unbroken left arm. As soon as you introduce a variable, the broken arm, into the swing, it becomes necessary to correct the error before the club

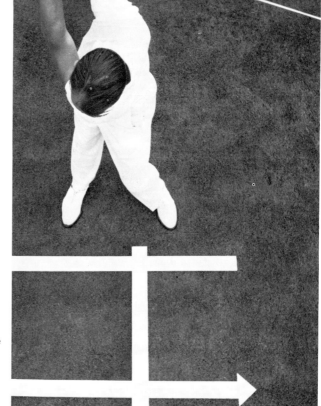

An excellent overhead view of Glenn at the top of his backswing. Note that his shoulders have turned considerably more than his hips, thus setting up the necessary tension between the lower body and the upper body. Note that his head has retained a steady position over the ball and yet has turned slightly to the right to accommodate his big shoulder turn. Note the evident tension in the right leg as the swing has wound up against it. This is what might be called a "picture swing" and is good evidence of why Glenn has been Michigan amateur champion five times.

can be returned to its original starting position.

The moral is—while you are learning this wonderful game—try to learn the most efficient way to hit the ball, the way that will lead to fewer variations and swing troubles that will have to be corrected later. Work on keeping your left arm *firm*. Its position is not one of rigidity because that state leads to excessive muscle tension, which will destroy your ability to swing smoothly and rhythmically. It is not loose but somewhere in between rigidity and looseness.

To achieve the correct feeling, try holding the club very loosely and hitting a few golf balls. You will find that the torque, or turning movement, imparted to the clubhead at impact with the ball has to be resisted with some degree of firmness in your left hand and arm. That is the degree of firmness you must maintain in your golf swing. It is an individual matter, one that you must work out for yourself.

Here, I am illustrating the fault of "laying off" at the top of the backswing. You can see that my left wrist has bent downward. This is a weak position and results in a very flat swing with the golfer's club around behind him rather than up high, above shoulder-level, where it should be.

The appearance of wrinkles in the flesh below my left wrist indicates a weaker wrist position at the top of the backswing. It leads to what is called a "shut face" of the club and is conducive to a closed face at impact, which often will cause a hook. Try to achieve a flat appearance at the top of your backswing. It is a stronger position and will work better for you in the long run.

Here is an example of my full but "three-quarter swing" with the driver. Note the full shoulder turn, with the left shoulder pointing at the ball, and the obvious tension in the left side and left shoulder as I wind up against my right foot, which is square to the line of flight. My head has turned slightly to the right to accommodate the shoulder turn, but my master eye, the left, remains fixed on the back of the ball.

chapter 10

RHYTHM AND BALANCE

According to the dictionary, "rhythm denotes the regular patterned flow, the ebb and rise of movements in physical activities." Rhythmical means "having rhythm, recurring with measured regularity." When we say that the golf swing must have rhythm and be rhythmical, we mean that each separate golf swing should have the same "regular patterned flow" from the moment the golfer steps into his stance and the golf swing begins until the golf ball is sent on its way and the swing comes to its natural conclusion. The term "rhythmical" applies to the consistent repetition of the same coordinated, measured golf swing time after time in an identical pattern, swing after swing.

This rhythmical swing is best seen in the great golfers of our day. One of the finest examples of a repeating, rhythmical swing in golf is that of the great champion, Gene Littler. Whether he is hitting a full drive, a medium iron, or a short pitch shot, he exhibits the same smooth, almost leisurely tempo in his swing. But the results he gets with his smooth swing pay off in a consistently high acceleration of clubhead speed and the resulting beautiful golf shots, long and accurate.

Horton Smith often said that, in his opinion, the golf swing could be likened to a dance step. He claimed that from the moment the golfer assumes his stance he should be thinking of the rhythm of music or of a dance. The golfer's body weight moves from left to right in rhythmic se-

Here is a sequence of three photos showing Horton Smith demonstrating his exercise to perfect the rhythm and balance of the golf swing. Horton recommended that the golfer either sing to himself mentally or find a rhythmic set of words to use in conjunction with the moves. One expression he suggested was, "One, two, three, Swiiiiiing!"

quence as he "feels" his proper balance from the soles of his feet up through his whole body. As this feeling of balance and rhythm pervades the entire body, the moment comes for a "forward press," a sort of push-off or kick-off that starts the club and the body into simultaneous motion in a smooth takeaway from the ball.

This action of forward press is a natural one and usually is evidenced by the golfer tightening his grip on the club, a movement of the left hand toward the left, or a movement of the right knee toward the ball. Then, the reverse action, the takeaway starts. If you pay particular attention the next time you watch the top golfers on a televised program, you might detect this forward press movement in their hands or in their bodies. For most players it is a completely unconscious maneuver, an instinctive one that does not re-

quire any particular attention of the mind. In my opinion, you do not need to think about your own forward press in your swing, but since you will hear discussions among golfers about the forward press, it is well that you know about it. You will make the move naturally, as all golfers do.

Your success at golf depends upon your ability to develop your own rhythmical swing. If you have been successful at other sports during your life and have played baseball, hockey, tennis, ping-pong, basketball, or even billiards with some skill, it is likely that your body already is trained to execute the rhythmical movements of the golf swing.

Here, Horton Smith is pictured executing what he called the "dance step" of the golf swing. You can and should imitate his movements. The result will be a better, more rhythmical motion.

This sequence shows Horton Smith demonstrating his idea of the "dance step" rhythm in the golf swing. Horton suggested swinging the club to music in order to improve rhythm.

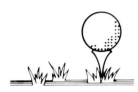

chapter 11
THE TOP OF THE BACKSWING

As we all know, the backswing in golf takes the club away from the ball and winds up the muscles of the body to a certain degree of tension. The bow and arrow in the pictures show various degrees of tension in the bow and, therefore, the power potential in the eventual release of the arrow. So, too, are you, the golfer, able to achieve various degrees of power in your backswing.

Basically, it would seem that the farther you bring your club backward in your swing, the more power you would get. This is not necessarily true. The fact is that there must be tension in the muscles of the body as a result of the greater winding up of the shoulder muscles in opposition to the muscles of the lower trunk, which lag behind the upper body in the backward turn.

You can prove this to yourself by a physical exercise. Stand with your feet in a slightly open golf stance. Place your right

foot at one o'clock, picturing a clock dial, and your left foot at eleven o'clock. Now turn your upper body as far as you can to the right in a mock golf backswing. You will feel a certain degree of tension, but note that it does not come into play until you are near the end of your body move.

For the second part of this demonstration, turn your right foot to a twelve o'clock position. You can leave your left foot at eleven o'clock or turn it to ten o'clock, as you wish. Try the same move again and you will notice at once the greater building of tension along the left side of your body, in your left leg, and especially in the muscles of your left waist and left back. This demonstration of the windup of the body with the right foot at twelve o'clock is also strong evidence and support for the proposition that in the modern golf swing the twelve o'clock right foot position gives more tension and, therefore,

more power to your swing. Observe Arnold Palmer's swing, Lee Trevino's swing, Hale Irwin's swing, and the swings of many other fine players and you will note that they, too, practice this principle of right foot tension-building.

Tension must be built into each swing for it to be successful. When the stretch of the arms and hands into the backswing does not reach far enough to the right to cause that lower left side tension, the swing is faulty. True, it may have some power, but it definitely will not have the maximum power that the golfer should be able to command.

Develop your backswing with the tension-building thought in mind. If you are young and supple, you may be able to get what is technically called a "big windup," one in which the left shoulder points to the ball or even to the right of the ball at the top of the backswing. Or, if you are less supple, you may end your backswing at what is known as the three-quarter position, a spot about three-quarters of the way to a "full" backswing.

You must find this "stop" spot in your backswing yourself. You will have to experiment on a practice tee. Try swings that allow you to bring the club back far enough for it to become parallel with the ground. Try swings that bring your hands to shoulder height only. Try swings in between these "stop" spots, but find it for yourself. What you are searching for is that point of maximum tension in your body, and once you have determined that spot, concentrate on getting to it with no longer a backswing and no shorter a backswing every time you swing.

I advise you to observe the good players' backswings. You will see young Ben Crenshaw use a backswing that takes the club several degrees beyond parallel, and you will see Doug Sanders with a backswing that appears to be no more than shoulder high.

Yet, each of these swings produces the maximum power for each of these golfers. In my own case, I found that curtailing my long backswing resulted in more consistently straight golf shots and, oddly enough, gave more power and length to my shots. All I can suggest is that you find your own "stop" spot at the top of your backswing.

chapter **12**

THE STOP AT THE TOP

You will find that if you are able to pinpoint that exact moment in your backswing where the club ceases its backward motion and begins to reverse itself, starts down on its way to the ball, you will have made a marvelous discovery about your golf swing, one that can and should give you great control.

This moment is known as the "stop" at the top of the backswing. In some good golfers this stop seems to last a full second or so. It is a distinctively individual part of their swings. Dr. Cary Middlecoff and Bob Murphy are two outstanding examples of definite pauses at the top of their backswings. Whether you can or cannot adopt a similar pause remains to be seen as you progress through your golf education. If you are able to do so, it will be useful. But, on the other hand, if you don't, don't worry about it. You can time your swing in some other way more natural to you, perhaps.

Obviously, in every swing there is a point at which the motion of the club must reverse itself. By practicing your swing with the left hand only, you should be able to zero in on that important fraction of a second in your swing. By maintaining a firm grip with the last three fingers of your left hand, you will have control over the distance the club is able physically to travel in its backward arc. If you allow these fin-

gers to relax, the weight and momentum of the club will force them to open. The result will be a loose, ineffectual swing, one that has the fault of "snatching" or re-closing the fingers on the club at the top of the swing. (See photo in Chapter 34.) This fault is one that completely destroys the rhythm of the swing and prevents the golfer from being aware of the stop at the top of his backswing.

A swing that is overly rapid will impart considerable momentum to the shaft and clubhead and will tend to apply more force against those last three fingers of the left hand than would be applied in a slower swing.

So if you want to build a sound, repeating, effective golf swing, work on sensing that moment of stop at the top of your backswing. Develop a leisurely, definitely not rapid swing. Once you discover the sensation of the stop, you will feel that daylight suddenly has dawned on your golf career. You will sense and feel great control over your swing, much like the control that an archer has when he draws back his arrow to a certain point and then releases it at exactly the point of tension he desires.

When you have learned to sense this "stop" point, you are ready to proceed to the next most important part of the golf swing—the release through the ball.

chapter **13**

THE START-DOWN AND THE LEFT SIDE PULL-DOWN

Here is the "moment of truth" in the golf swing! Granted, the impact of the clubhead on the ball is certainly the most important "moment of moments" in golf. Still, the reversal of the swing at the top, the "start-down" toward the ball, is, in my opinion, the "moment of truth" in the swing. If it is done in proper fashion, every other motion in the golf swing flows in beautiful rhythmic sequence: the clubhead accelerates to its greatest speed just as it reaches the impact area; the right hand and arm speed up and square up the face of the clubhead; and the ball is struck fairly on the face of the club at an exact right angle to the line toward the target. The result is a functionally good and true golf swing, a ball sent speeding on its way toward the flagstick.

It is most important that you understand that "trigger point" in your swing that starts your clubhead on its way back down to the ball. The emphasis must be placed on left-sidedness at this crucial point. Your swing has moved a portion of your weight to the right-hand side of your body. You have "wound up" the muscles of your arms, shoulders, and trunk to the fullest extent possible.

Now! Pull down with your entire left side. Resist any temptations to begin to hit the ball with your right hand and arm. I assure you that your right hand and right arm "hit" will be there at the moment of impact if you will obey this rule: "Start your downswing with a left-side move." For the beginner, it will be best to think of this left-side move as trying to strike the golf ball back handed, that is, with the left hand only. You may even consider the mental imagery of a left-handed backhand shot in the game of tennis if that will help to impress on your mind the proper thought and action.

As this pull-down with your left arm and left side occurs, you will find that those muscles of your body so carefully coiled in the backswing are suddenly sprung loose, freed, and ready to help accelerate the golf club and clubhead down the return path to and through the ball at the impact area.

I personally do not like the use of the term "impact area" or, as it is sometimes called, "hitting area" because I believe those terms connote a feeling of "hit" rather than the idea of an action that flows through the area where the ball merely "happens" to be in the way of the club. Horton Smith often said that the golfer should imagine that he is swinging his clubhead through a puff of smoke, that he will find no resistance whatsoever at the bottom of the swing, that the golf ball just happens to be in the way of the clubhead and will be sent on its path almost by the accident of being there. Horton also likened the smoothness and acceleration of

the downswing to the motion of a car that "takes off" from a stoplight and, without changing gears, accelerates to top speed. He also said that the unrhythmic swing could be likened to the same car shifting gears halfway to its final acceleration speed. We all know the hesitation that occurs before the car regains its original accelerating momentum.

There are two mental pictures you can use to train yourself to perform this left-handed maneuver that begins the downswing. The thought that I prefer, because it has worked effectively for me for many years, is that I am pulling my left arm downward toward my left side. I find that the rest of my body obeys this command with the necessary counterclockwise rotation of my lower body, which in turn brings the clubhead down and through the ball with suitable acceleration.

The other thought, one that Horton Smith often advised his pupils to use if they had difficulty understanding and executing the left side pull-down, was to think of leaving your left hand, left arm, and the clubhead at the top of the swing, completely forgetting about them there, and concentrating upon the area of your right pocket, thinking, "I will turn my right pocket back to the ball as quickly as I can." Of course, this counterclockwise motion of the lower body is exactly the same as the left side pull-down concept just explained.

You should experiment with both of these "trigger thoughts" to see which one works best for you. Chances are strong that you will prefer the left side pull-down theory because it may be easier for you to execute. Remember that your mind can hold only one thought at a time. The left hand pull-down thought and the thought of rotating the right-hand pocket back toward the ball are both single, positive thoughts. If you will concentrate on using either one in your game, you will discover that you have been able to block out of your mind any thought of failure in the swing.

A very important benefit that flows from the "left side pull-down" theory is that it plays down the role of the right hand in the swing. This is most useful because, since most of us are right-handed, we in- stinctively want to apply our right-handed power to the swing, inevitably too soon or in such a manner that the left hand is un- able to withstand the force of the right- hand "hit" and collapses at impact, with the bad result of a mis-hit golf shot, a dreadful slice, or an awful hook.

Here is a marvelous stop-action photo of Glenn Johnson just as his hands and wrists are about to release their power at the ball. Note how he has already "cleared his left side," proving that he moved it down and through the ball very early in his downswing. See how his right elbow is close to his right side, the excellent, steady position of his head over the ball, and the wrists still cocked but just about ready to release their power for maximum acceleration of the clubhead against the ball.

This is Glenn's swing a fraction of a second before he strikes the ball. Note that his weight is entirely on his left side. It has been there since the start of the downswing. His right elbow is tight against his body, which allows the swing to stay inside the line to the target and eventually square the clubface at impact. Observe, too, Glenn's shoulder "tilt," or shoulder plane, which allows his right shoulder to come under his chin. Glenn has held his head steady over the ball and will not allow it to come up until the right side of his chin brings it up in his full follow through.

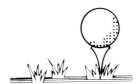

chapter **14**

THE RELEASE THROUGH THE BALL

We have discussed the first move from the top of the backswing, the left side pull-down. The golfer's hips start to "clear" to the left. The left side of the body, which has been so tightly coiled on the back-swing, now uncoils and allows the left hand and left wrist to release through the ball in a backhand manner. At the same time, the right hand, right wrist, right elbow, and right arm are trying to keep up with the action of the left hand and left side. Ideally, at the moment the club reaches the ball, there is a "tied race" between the left and right hands, the right finally catching up to the left and squaring the clubface at impact.

It is this moment of impact that is called the release *through* the ball, for both hands act together, essentially as one. The power released by the right hand as it speeds up and squares up the clubface must be just enough, neither more nor less than the power required of the left hand to brace itself to withstand not only the torque of the hit but also the power of the right hand. It is for this reason that we place so much emphasis on exercises that strengthen both hands, particularly the left. The more strength you can build in your left hand, left wrist, and left arm, the more power you will be able to apply with your right

without ever "overcoming" the left. For your right hand must *never* pass the left as it hits through the ball.

The proper release of the hands through the ball, is, of course, the heart of the golf game. Master the timing here so that both hands act as one and your golf swing is on its way to success!

This is an excellent example of a good follow through after a drive. It is clear that my left hand has not "broken down," that the right hand has not "passed the left." My head has remained steady over the ball. There is no question but that this hand and swing action will result in a straight, accurate golf shot.

A side view of Glenn Johnson in his magnificent follow through. See how his weight is entirely on his left side. He has cleared his left side so far that his body actually is pointing to the left of the target. Note, too, how his head has remained in a steady position, but that his right shoulder has forced it up slightly as the follow through continued to completion.

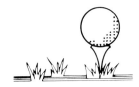

chapter 15

THE FINISH

We have come to the final fundamental of a sound golf swing: standing tall at the finish. The phrase "standing tall" is meant to convey a feeling of free release of all the energy that has been exerted in the golf swing, of a full body turn through the hit, or impact, area, of no "stop" in the left side of the body, left leg, left arm, left hand, or left wrist as the swing continued to completion.

The phrase "standing tall at the finish" also should convey to you a mirror image of your swing as you reached the top of your backswing. The muscles of your trunk, legs, and arms, once tightly spring-coiled, now have been released, and the hit and "swing through" have been accomplished. The hands have smashed through the impact zone against the braced strength of the left leg, left side, left arm, and firmed left wrist. There is a feeling of completeness, of fulfillment. The purpose of the golf swing has been accomplished. The tension in the body until the moment of impact finally has been dissipated as the swing has come to a rested halt.

The golfer's hands and arms swing through the ball and come to a stop at shoulder height or even higher if the force of the swing carries enough momentum.

An excellent thought when beginning your swing is, "I already can see myself in the successful follow through. I will stand tall at the finish."

Another view, from head-on, of Glenn Johnson completing his full follow through. Note how high his hands are above his head, and yet his head is still back, behind the ball, which is now in flight.

Here is my swing at shoulder height. Note that my hands and wrists are still in the same aspect that they were at the takeaway position. This is called a "delayed wrist cock." My wrists begin to break, or "cock," between this spot and the top of my swing. In order to increase the compactness of my swing, I have found it useful to hold my backswing to no higher than the three-quarter point. If you are supple enough, you may find it useful to take your swing all the way to the "parallel to the ground" point.

chapter 16

THE MYTH OF THE STRAIGHT BALL

I have been watching the best golfers in the world for more than forty years. I have seen their swings on the practice tees of more than ten Master's tournaments at Augusta, Georgia, as well as in about fifteen Open championships. Of these hundreds of players, there are only two that I ever saw hit the ball dead straight consistently. Those two golfers were Cary Middlecoff and Ben Hogan. Later, even Hogan decided he would "fade" the ball for better control, that is, move it from left to right with clockwise spin.

My point is this: every golfer puts some spin on the ball, which causes it to curve in flight. If the clubhead moves from an inside line to an outside line, the movement of the clubface across the ball will cause it to spin off with counterclockwise motion. That ball will hook. If the clubhead moves from an outside line to an inside line, the

movement of the clubface will cause a clockwise spin on the ball. That ball will slice.

The violence or amount of the spin imparted depends for the most part on the angle at which the clubface hits the ball. But it also is affected by the hand and wrist action of the golfer at impact, which can put additional spin on the ball.

In the final analysis, in order to hit a perfectly straight ball it is necessary:

1) to have a swing that allows the clubface to strike the ball when the clubface is absolutely square to the target line; and

2) to have a swing that allows the clubface to stay on that square line for the fraction of a second during which the ball and the clubface remain in contact before the ball leaves the clubface and springs into flight.

These are the "go" and "no go" takeaway positions. Depending upon the ability of the golfer to take his club straight away from the ball, the takeaway line will be directly away from the ball on the target line or else on the inside of that line, as shown above. A takeaway outside that line in the "no" area of this photograph leads to an ineffective swing from the outside-in and should be avoided.

Glenn is demonstrating his excellent "one-piece" takeaway. Note that although his club has traveled several feet into his backswing, his hands and wrists remain in the same unbroken position they were in at the start of his swing. His shoulders have begun to turn, and his lower body is beginnig to wind up against the resistance of his right leg and right side. His head remains steady over the ball although he has allowed it to turn slightly to the right to facilitate his big shoulder turn.

This means that the golfer should adopt a swing pattern that takes his clubface away from the ball in a position square to his target line and returns it there, as well.

You will observe good golfers, as I have observed them, and you will see that their swings take their clubheads either straight away from the ball or slightly inside the line. Never do you see a good golfer take his clubhead away from the ball outside the line to his target.

The photos should be studied carefully. I have indicated "go" and "no go" areas for your takeaway. I cannot tell you exactly where in the "go" section you will find your swing pattern. A great deal depends upon your own ability to develop the "all-in-one-piece" takeaway. If your body, hands, and arms all move at the takeaway in one single motion and if you do not break your wrists too soon in the backswing, your swing pattern should find your club coming directly away and square to the ball and target for perhaps a foot or so of the backswing. On the other hand, if your swing pattern is not completely "all-in-one-piece," if your wrist break occurs earlier in the swing, and if your body turn to the right happens at the same time, your club will come inside that square-to-the-target line. Don't worry about it if you find that your backswing is inside the line. Most good golfers do have swings that

bring the clubhead inside the line.

But do *not* let your backswing get outside the line if you possibly can avoid it. If you do, you undoubtedly will be cursed with the duffer's terrible problem of slicing. The takeaway outside the line, in addition to failing to move the lower body in a proper turn, results in the clubhead eventually striking the ball from outside-to-inside. This type of contact spins the ball clockwise and gives you that horror of horrors, the slice.

As your game develops, you will find that you are either a consistent slicer or a consistent hooker. For a while in your early game, before you standardize your style, you might hook and slice on successive shots. Don't worry about it. Just work on making your swing the same every time. Standardization will come and with it consistency in striking the ball with one type of spin or the other.

As all good golfers do, you will "work with the hook" or you will "work with the slice." You will learn to aim slightly to the right of the target if you hook, slightly to the left of the target if you slice.

And the next time you watch the good golfers in action, try to figure out in advance which way they are going to "work" the ball, hook it or slice it. Remember these sage words: "Nobody hits the golf ball perfectly straight!"

The one-third power swing is often used on chip and pitch shots around the green. If you will picture the same club taken back so that it points over the right shoulder, you will have an idea of the two-thirds point for two-thirds power.

chapter 17

THE ONE-THIRD SWING

The "one-third swing" is exactly what its name implies, a swing with one-third power. It is executed with a backswing one-third as long as the full power swing and one-half as long as the two-thirds swing, which found your backswing at shoulder to head height.

The one-third swing will be used at distances from 100 yards in to the green if you are a powerful golfer or from the 60- to 70-yard distance if you are less than powerful. Once again, I repeat that you are to be the master of your own swing. You are the only person who can decide at what distance your swing power will be reduced from full power to two-thirds to one-third power.

Here is the way to find your one-third swing. Let us presume that you already have found the full power and two-thirds power target areas with your 5-iron. We will continue to presume that 100 yards is the distance you consistently hit your two-thirds power 5-iron. Now, bring that target down to 50 yards. Continue to use your 5-iron to strike the ball that distance. At

first you will naturally over-hit the target, but as you practice, the one-third concept will sink into your mind, and you eventually will be able to hit the 5-iron with a considerably shortened backswing. That swing, which most golfers find for this one-third-power shot, stops about belt-high in the backswing and takes the ball the one-third distance you are seeking.

For this swing, your left foot is drawn even more away from the line of flight to the target. This further opening of your stance will constrict your backswing to a greater degree than the two-thirds swing did. Your weight will remain primarily on your left side during this swing to ensure a stroke that goes down and through the ball.

The two physical facts, the wider open stance and the greater predominance of weight on the left side of your body, will give you an excellent one-third swing. This is the swing you will use for your shots around the green, approaches with lofted irons over bunkers or water, short chips and pitches, and for the delicate shots that must land close to the hole.

chapter **18**

THE TWO-THIRDS SWING

Thus far we have discussed the full and one-third swing. The full swing is the most important, of course, and will be employed in probably 75 percent of your game. However, it is obvious that when you begin to come near to your target green, you will need to use a swing that will take the golf ball a shorter distance than if you hit with your complete windup and full swing.

Your full swing takes your club, at the top of your backswing, to a position parallel to the ground; usually with your hands high above your head even if the club does not reach the position parallel to the ground. Think of your full swing as assembled from two parts, one part is the two-thirds swing and the other the one-third swing. Having discussed the one-third swing, let's turn now to the two-thirds swing.

The two-thirds backswing will bring your club to about shoulder height. When do you employ the two-thirds backswing? You and you alone must make that decision. You will have to work with your game to determine which clubs give you less power and distance.

I suggest that for a start you consider your 5-iron as the "breaking off" point. You should be able to find out whether it is or not by working on the practice tee. Hit about twenty full shots with your 5-iron. Then, pick a spot on the range about two-thirds the distance of the full shot. It will be wise to pace off that distance and mark it with some sort of target. A cluster of golf balls may do the trick. Don't take your longest 5-iron shot, but find the spot where most of your 5-iron shots cluster. Let's say, for example, that that distance is 150 yards. In that event, your two-thirds target is 100 yards distant. If your 5-iron full shot travels only 140 yards, your two-thirds shot would be in the 90-yard range.

Your swing must be shortened to accomplish the two-thirds swing. This shortening may be done in two ways. First, open your stance several inches by drawing your left foot counterclockwise away from the line of flight. Your left toe will be pointing more toward the target than it does for the full shot. Be careful not to turn your upper body away at the same time, just your lower body, which will turn naturally to the left in response to the left foot position. You will keep more of your weight on your left side in this two-thirds swing than you did in your full swing. The open stance will help to accomplish this because it will cause the muscles of your left side to become taut more quickly than in the full swing. This physical restriction will assist you in finding your two-thirds backswing.

Second, you must locate the stopping point in your backswing that will give you two-thirds of your full power swing. You will have to experiment with your swing and find it for yourself. It is possible that this point is reached when your hands are head height or, possibly, when they are shoulder high. You will know the answer when you consistently are able to hit those

5-iron shots to the 100-yard target area.

Once you have made this discovery, you are on your way to becoming a complete golfer because every good golfer must have in his repertory many swings of less than full power. You will need them in situations where the distance to the target is less than the full power range of the club used. Later, as your game develops, you may experiment with the two-thirds swing with clubs longer than the 5-iron—your 3-iron, 5-wood, or 3-wood. But at the start, learn to hit your 5-iron with the two-thirds swing, and then practice with your more lofted irons all the way down to your pitching wedge.

It is important, too, that you learn just how far you are able to hit your 5-iron (or any other club, for that matter) with your full swing and how far you can hit with your two-thirds swing. This knowledge will give you a great deal of confidence in your game. Your swing, you will find, is adaptable to many different situations.

Most beginner golfers are under the impression that one and only one golf club is meant to be used to strike the golf ball a certain distance. This definitely is not the case. As you work with your game and learn the "two-thirds, one-third" concept, you will come to realize that there may be as many as two or even three different clubs that can be used with success for any given distance.

Here is an example. We will presume that your full swing with your 5-iron takes the ball comfortably to the 150-yard target. You also may find, as you practice your two-thirds swing, that your 3-iron will take it 150 yards. Now, you have the option of using either the 3-iron or the 5-iron for that distance. If you are making that 150-yard shot into a strong headwind, it might be more practical to use the 3-iron instead of the 5-iron to keep the ball closer to the ground in its flight, where it will be less influenced by the wind.

Understanding how to use the two-thirds swing may not come for quite a while in your golf game. But it will come if you adopt these practice suggestions. First, think "two-thirds" swing. That is, consciously try to exert two-thirds of the force you customarily use in your full swing. Second, open your stance moderately by moving your left foot away from the target line, more to the left of the target. Be careful, though, to keep your upper body on line toward the target. Third, consciously limit your backswing to your own two-thirds length, the length at which you can execute a shot that will travel two-thirds the distance of a full shot with the same club. Practice!

The clubface angle with the driver.

The clubface angle with the 3-wood.

The clubface angle with the 5-iron.

chapter 19
MATHEMATICS OF THE CLUBFACE ANGLE

Golf is a mathematical game. Golf clubs are designed to drive a golf ball at precise angles into the air. Just as a ray of light is reflected at a right angle from a mirror, so, too, does the golf ball spring off the clubface at a right angle to the angle the clubface makes with the ground. Pictured are views of the driver, the 3-wood, the 5-iron, and the 9-iron, which clearly show that the ball will be driven from the faces of the clubs at angles of 11°, 16°, 32°, and 48°, respectively. Understanding the mathematics of the clubface will lead to the realization that the golfer does not need to "help" the club do its work of lofting the ball. He merely needs to strike the ball and let the mathematical factor of rebound give him the proper result.

The clubface angle with the 9-iron.

This is the putting stance in which the right foot is drawn back from the target line. This style is very useful for keeping the blade on the inside and for avoiding "cutting" the putt, that is, imparting a spin from left to right. This putting style was made famous by A. D. "Bobby" Locke, the great African star of golf, who is said to have hooked all of his putts—right into the hole. Gary Player often is seen putting in this stance.

CHAPTER 20
THE PUTTING STROKE

Today I know of many golfers who are only second- or third-rate golfers, but whose skill as putters is all that keeps them in the rank that they do hold . . . My personal opinion is that more men are good putters from practice than because they have any pronounced superiority, to begin with, over other men.

Francis Ouimet
United States Open Golf Champion, 1913
United States Amateur Golf Champion, 1914

There are, basically, three styles of putting stroke, the all-wrist method, the all-arm method, and the arm-wrist method, which is a compromise between the other two methods.

You will see an infinite variety of putting styles if you watch either the golfers of the professional world or the everyday country club or public links golfers. In the accompanying photos are examples of the open stance, the closed stance, and the feet-on-line stance, which you will see most often. Jack Nicklaus practices a style that puts his right foot closer to the putting line than his left. Gary Player does the reverse; he keeps his right foot behind his left foot. Al Geiberger is a noted example of the golfer who keeps his feet precisely in line, parallel with the line of the putt.

There are certain fundamentals observed by all good putters no matter what method of putting they use. They include, first, a steady platform of body, legs, and arms. That means, for the most part, that the body is crouched somewhat, with the weight mainly on the left foot and left side of the body. The head is either directly over the ball at a right angle that runs from the hole to the ball to the golfer's eye, or else the head is held in a position over the ball but slightly behind it, as though the golfer were sighting from ball to cup. Another consistent practice of good putters is keeping the clubhead close to the ground in backswing and in forward swing. In order to do this successfully, it is necessary to use the combination arm-and-wrist movement. And that is probably the reason why about 75 percent of all golfers use this method.

Billy Casper is an outstanding example of the wrist putting method, and left-hander Bob Charles is acknowledged to be the best "arm-putter" in the world. Putting experts are of the opinion that both all-wrist and all-arm methods are less controllable at medium- and long-distance putting—but with the perfection one sees in Casper and Charles, who can say?

Since I putt using the Horton Smith arm-wrist method and have always putted well with it, I recommend that you try this method before you go to one of the rarer styles, the all-arm or the all-wrist method. However, by all means, use the putting stroke that feels most natural to you.

THE FUNDAMENTALS OF A GOOD PUTTING STROKE

Here are the fundamentals of the arm-wrist method of putting as taught by Horton Smith. (Note: The entire textbook by Horton Smith and Dawson Taylor is published by A.S. Barnes and Company under the title *The Secret of Holing Putts* and by Wilshire Publishing in paperback as *The Secret of Perfect Putting*.)

1. A proper grip is the key to the two important principles of keeping the blade of the putter "square" and stroking the blade low and level to the turf.

2. There are two secrets to keeping the blade of the putter "square" and stroking low and level to the turf: a) "hooding" with the left wrist; and b) "arching" both the right and left wrists.

3. Along with a proper grip and knowl-

edge of the two secrets, "hooding" and "arching," there should be a thorough understanding of the "box" principle and "squareness to the line."

4. The golfer should have the ability to make an effective survey of the green. This requires good eyesight, a vivid imagination, and an ability to recall all previous experiences in both actual play and practice.

5. Finally, the golfer must have a confident and positive attitude when he approaches a putt. This requires concentration, relaxation, and control of the nerves—assets that are best developed by the recollection of the physical action of previous successful putting.

Horton Smith is demonstrating his theory of the "Box Principle" and squareness to the putting line. You, too, can use a yardstick and a ruler to impress upon your mind the theory and the practice of the "square-to-the-line" putting stroke.

"Hooding" is the term given to the necessary counterclockwise turn of the left wrist during the backswing of the putting stroke. A slight rotation is applied in order to keep the blade of the putter constantly "square to the line" of the putt.

"Arching" refers to the positioning of the wrists in a downward curve so that you will tend to utilize only the back-and-forth hinges of the wrists. The photo gives a visual representation of the putter blade at a right angle to the proposed line of the putt. Note that the putter blade is parallel and laid at a right angle to the putting line. The blade should stay at a right angle throughout the putting stroke. The hands attempt to keep the blade in a constantly square position, even after the ball has been struck. In the follow through, the blade should be kept low to the turf and no "break" should occur in the left wrist. At the same time, the back of the left hand as well as the palm of the right hand should stay at a right angle to the line of the putt.

Here is Horton Smith demonstrating his theory of right angles in putting. He felt that the line to the cup and the line from the ball in toward the golfer's left shoe were true right angles and that the golfer should visualize them as such in order to help him stroke the ball down the line.

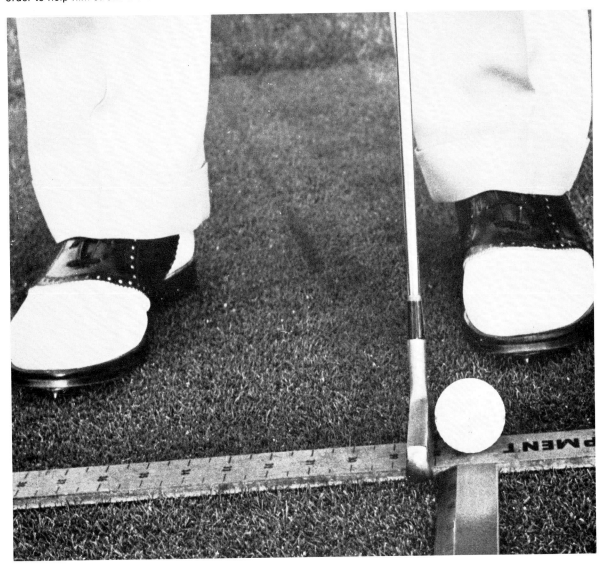

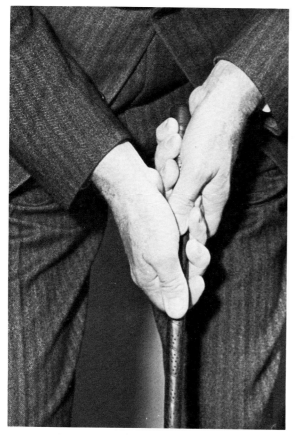

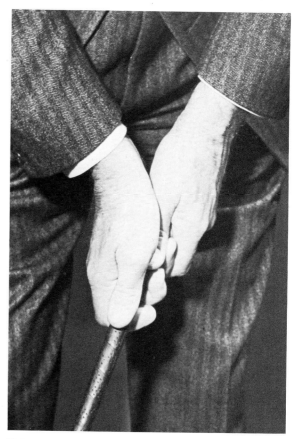

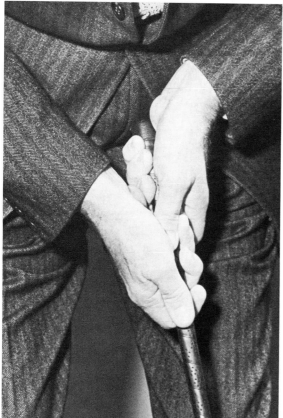

This is Horton Smith demonstrating his putting stroke. *(Above, left)*, the starting position. *(Above, right)*, the backswing. *(Left)*, the forward swing. Note the arched left wrist and the definite arm-wrist action.

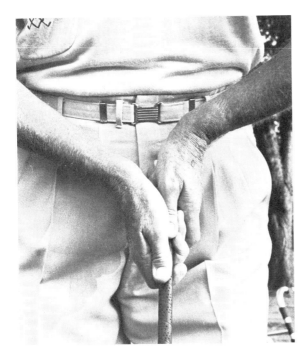

Horton Smith is demonstrating his famous putting grip. Note the reverse overlapping grip of the left hand with the two thumbs directly down the shaft and the elbow pointing toward the hole.

The Smith arm-wrist method also is based upon an understanding of what Horton called the "Box Principle." The basic point of it is squareness. The feet, the hips, the shoulders, and the hands all must be square to the putting line. The key is the hand position: the back of the left hand and the palm of the right hand must always face directly toward the hole at the beginning of the stroke, at impact, and during the follow through. Smith also claimed that he had a low, level-to-the-turf stroke, which kept the putter head low going back and required no adjustment for the forward stroke. He claimed that such a stroke allowed him to give his complete attention to "feeling" and concentrating upon the stroke itself and that his low, or level blade, method produced the most sensitive stroke and an overspinning ball that "hunts the cup."

This is the so-called "reverse" putting grip used by a large percentage of golfers. Note that the overlap is reversed so that the forefinger of the left hand fits into the slot between the last two fingers of the right hand. The idea of this grip is to let the right hand control the stroke and yet retain a feeling of solidity and unity in the hands.

The reverse putting grip—Arnold Palmer style—is a modification of the grip used by many good putters. The left forefinger is placed outside of the right hand in a sort of brace to prevent breaking the left wrist at impact. It is also a very solid grip that gives a desired predominance to the stroking right hand. Arnold Palmer has made this grip well known.

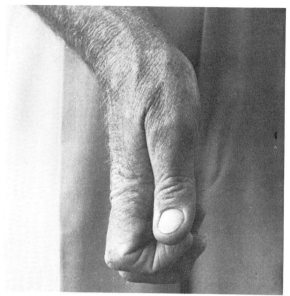

Here is Horton Smith demonstrating the position of the right hand alone in the proper putting grip. Again, note the straight line of the back of the hand, the squareness to the intended line. His thumb is directly on top of the shaft in a very delicate touch. Most of his feeling, he claimed, was centered in the fingers and particularly in the "pad" of the right forefinger, which should be imagined as having a plane of glass passed through it and all the bones of the back of the right hand. Furthermore, that plane of glass is at a perfect right angle to the intended line of the putt.

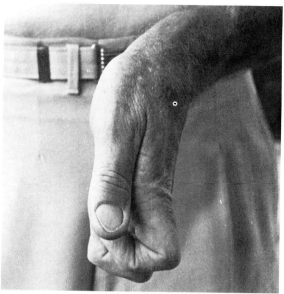

A view of Horton Smith demonstrating the proper left-hand grip for putting with the arm-wrist method that he taught so successfully. Note the squareness of the back of his hand to the intended line of the putt. Once again there should be a feeling that a plane of glass has been passed through the back of the left hand and that it extends through the pad, or third section, of the forefinger of the left hand at a perfect right angle to the line of the putt.

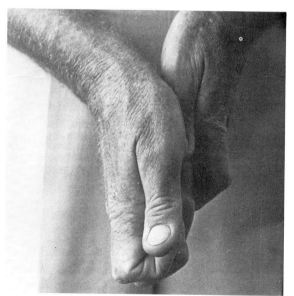

Horton Smith with both of his hands applied to an imaginary club. Note that his two thumbs are directly down the shaft in order to add to the feeling of squareness to the line. Horton also recommended that reverse "Vardon grip" in which the forefinger of the left hand lightly overlaps the little finger of the right hand. He claimed that it added to the right-handedness of the stroke and allowed more "feel" in the fingers of the right hand.

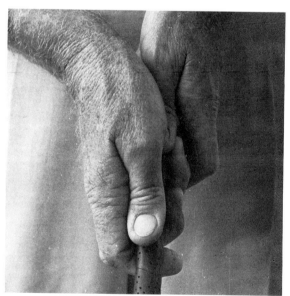

Here is a close-up shot of Horton Smith's grip applied to the shaft of a putter.

away. Or think of the way a boomerang sails out on a cushion of air and curves back gracefully to the hands of the thrower. These are the pictures to keep in mind when you think of the break of a green.

Here is a photo of my backswing on a long putt. Notice that the clubface has opened only slightly, indicating the hooding of the clubface action that has taken place in the left hand and left wrist as they took the club away from the ball. Compare this photo with others to mark the difference between heights of backswing in the all-wrist method and this arm-and-wrist method. The clubhead stays closer to the ground in the arm-wrist method and thus returns to the ball with less chance of error.

THE PUTTING SURVEY

"How far do you think this putt will break?" is an expression you will hear often on the green. The player asks his caddie or his partner and soon both of them are attempting to "solve" the problem of getting the ball into the hole over a sloping green. Here are three concepts of "borrow" and "break" on the golf green. (For example, you may "borrow" six inches from the left because the putt will "break" six inches from left to right.)

Picture steel balls in a pinball machine rolling up a slope and then down one side or the other. Or think of the banked corners around the Indianapolis Speedway, where the racers go high up into the corners and then come down into the straight-

This is the feet-on-line style of putting that many golfers adopt. The weight is primarily on the left side of the body, the head directly over the ball. This photo also illustrates the low-to-the-ground backswing and the hooded face of the putter, which is still square-to-the-line. This picture was posed to illustrate these points. In actual play the putter would be slightly raised above the turf.

This is my own putting stance with my right foot slightly advanced toward the line. My right elbow hugs my upper body, my left elbow is pointed directly toward the hole, and my head and eyes are directly over the ball, which is on a line off the inside of my left foot. Note that I do not change my normal Vardon grip when putting. It's just that I never have felt comfortable with the changed grip.

An ideal finish of the arm-wrist putting stroke. You should imagine that your blade is still square to your putting line even though the ball has been gone for several seconds. If the blade is square when it has finished the stroke, it had to be square at impact. Remember, this is an idealized position. Your club will be off the ground in actual play. But the idea you should bear in mind as you stroke the putt is to keep your blade square to the line "through the ball."

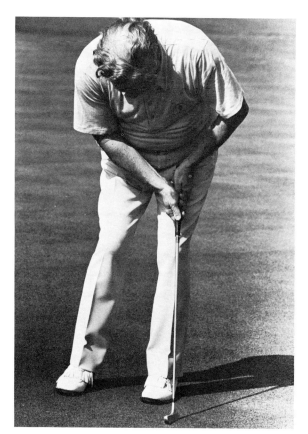

The wrist method of putting *(above, left)*. The idea is to let the putter act like a pendulum and return to the same spot at the bottom of the arc every time. Many good putters have used this method successfully. Billy Casper is an outstanding example and is considered one of the best putters of all time. The method takes a tremendous amount of practice to perfect.

The follow through for the wrist putting method *(above, right)*. Note how high the club must be taken in both backswing and follow through. Horton Smith always claimed that raising the club added another dimension to the stroke, and he believed that any body movement during the stroke prevented its successful completion.

Here is another popular putting style. Gary Player places his right foot away from the line of the putt. This is an excellent style for the player who is in the habit of slicing his putts as the stroke is almost forced on line or comes slightly from the inside to the outside of the line. The left arm pointing toward the hole is another excellent idea that is found in many putting styles. Lou Graham also exaggerates pointing his left arm toward the hole.

When making the survey for a 15-foot putt, I prefer to stand midway between the ball and the hole, keeping the ball on my right, the hole on my left, and trying to "see" the line the ball will take to the cup. This is merely a personal idiosyncrasy. You may prefer to look at the putt from both sides of the line, from behind and from below the putt. Whatever routine you develop, stick to it for every putt, even the short ones.

When measuring your putts, always walk to the side of, never on, your own putting line. Be careful to step over the putting lines of the other players as you count your paces from your own ball to the cup or from the cup to the ball. Do not walk on the last three paces nearest the cup but merely estimate them. You may put some unnecessary spike marks around the cup if you do. Register the total distance in your mind in round figures such as "a 40-footer," "a 35-footer," etc.

This is a survey for a 40-foot putt. I find it useful to "triangulate" the distance, that is, imagine the putting line as a triangle with its base the line to the hole. Then I estimate how strong my stroke must be to take the ball halfway to the hole and then all the way to the hole. By standing to one side, too, you are able to see the undulations in the green better than from behind the hole.

PUTT ON A SLOPING GREEN

Suppose you have a 20-foot putt on a green that is banked higher on the right than the left. Obviously, you will have to hit that putt off to the right of the straight line to the cup from the ball. Learning how much to borrow and trusting your judgment will only come with long experience. In general, the beginner golfer refuses to admit that the ball will break as much as his eye tells him it will. The result is a putt that either falls off short or to the "wrong" side of the cup. The "right" side, or professional side, of the cup is the side that is higher, where there is a better chance that the ball will fall into the cup if it comes close.

When lining up a putt, it might help to think of Horton Smith's quip: "All putts are straight . . . sometimes the cup isn't where it should be!"

By that he meant that the golfer should pretend that he is putting straight no matter how much the putt will break on the green. He should align himself with a system of right angles and "squareness to the line," the line toward that imaginary cup to the right or left of the actual cup, depending upon the amount of break. The beginner often is tempted to orient his body toward the cup even on severely breaking putts. Don't do it. Have confidence in your ability to see the proper line, and stroke your ball along it. You will have great satisfaction in solving breaking-putt problems, especially the extremely difficult ones. And practice, practice, practice!

The most important putt in golf, in my opinion, is the three-foot putt. Therefore, it is my recommendation that you practice making putts of that distance until you can look forward to making them nearly every time instead of dreading them as so many golfers do.

In his book *Golfer's Gold,* the late Tony

You should make a good percentage of your putts in the 10-foot range. The actual number will depend upon your own skill in developing a sound, repeating putting stroke and, of course, lots of practice. It is wise to stoop down behind the ball, directly in line with the hole, in order to spot any small, hidden rolls around the cup. Once you have made up your mind on your line, never change it in the act of taking your stroke or you will surely mis-hit the putt. Always try to be "up" to the hole, but don't "charge it." The cup is wider for a ball that dies at the cup.

Horton Smith demonstrating a useful trick in determining the slope of a green and the line of a putt. He advocated getting well off the green behind the ball so that the overall contour and "tilt" of the green could be better seen. If this action requires you to get down into a bunker, do not be afraid to do so. You can always rake the bunker after you have made your survey.

Lema tells about being in desperation about his putting and how he appealed to the great teacher, Horton Smith, for help. Here are Tony's own words about the situation:

At the beginning of 1961, I ran into a severe case of the putting jitters. I had started taking between 38 and 40 putts per round. I was never able to hole a 4-footer for a par. It occurred to me that Detroit was the home of Horton Smith, one of the game's great putters. I dialed his number and soon he was on the line. "Hello, Mr. Smith," I said. "This is Tony Lema. My putting is shot to pieces. I was hoping that you might be able to help me." "Absolutely," he said. "You come right on over." I drove over to Horton's club, and for an hour we practiced on the putting green. Horton explained that putting was almost entirely a right-handed stroke and that the left hand was there only to help keep the blade on line. He demonstrated an extremely helpful exercise. This involved holding the putter with nothing but my right hand and hitting the ball at the hole from 2 feet, then 4 feet, then 6, and finally 10 feet. My stroke came back. It was a miracle.

Because I frequently practiced putting at noon at the nearby Detroit Golf Club, I was aware that Tony Lema had come to consult with Horton Smith about his putting. Consequently, I had even greater interest in Tony's subsequent successful golf career. The putting techniques and practice methods that Horton Smith taught Tony Lema are the same ones I pass on to you now.

Each time you practice putting, take one golf ball and place it about one foot from the hole. With your right hand on the putter shaft and with your forefinger extended down the side of the shaft, place the blade behind the ball and gently *push* the ball into the hole. Of course, a push is not a legitimate golf stroke, and you must never use it on the golf course for fear of incurring a penalty. But as Horton found, the act of pushing the ball in this way impresses upon the golfer's intelligence and his subconscious mind that the ball must be *rolled* into the hole and that the blade must remain square to the intended putting line at all times, from the moment of impact by the blade until the ball is on its way to the hole. As you perform this exercise, you quickly will find that if you let the blade turn either in clockwise or counterclockwise fashion as it is performing this "push," the ball will not go straight.

Horton demonstrating the one-handed putting exercise that he advocated and that was so useful in improving the putting of Tony Lema.

Next, try this same style of push shot with the left hand only (the grip is normal, without forefinger extended). Once more it will become clear that for the stroke to be successful, the left hand must follow through with the left wrist in an unbroken position. Eventually, you should be able to hole every putt from the one-foot distance.

Then, start to move the ball farther away from the cup, to two feet, to three feet, and even farther. As you may remember from the anecdote about Lema, Horton had Tony putting one-handed at ten-foot distances.

Once you have acquired this sense of the importance of the right-hand stroke and the firm foundation of the left, you may begin to practice your own two-handed putting method.

I recommend that you use five golf balls—all brand new, all by the same manufacturer. I prefer to use Acushnet Titleist wound-balls because I can put them down on the green with the imprinted name along the line of the putt and watch to see whether or not I am rolling the ball precisely down its "equator." Incidentally, when you see professional golfers marking their short putts, it is usually for this same reason. They want that ball in exactly the proper alignment so that they can see it roll end-over-end.

With five balls in use during putting practice, you will find that you don't overload the cup as you putt into it. That is, all five can be holed one on top of the other without the last one protruding from the cup. Begin to figure and record your "odds" as you putt so that you know exactly what your chances are of holing the three-foot, the four-foot, and eventually the ten-foot putt. As you practice putting from longer distances, you also should understand the odds on putting your ball within a two- or three-foot range of the cup.

I believe that it is useful to play putting games as you practice. There are many games, obviously, but the ones I suggest here are not only good games but also great for putting practice.

Some of the games you can play alone are of the "how many out of ten" variety. In these games you take your five balls and find a smooth track to the cup. You might want to work on right-to-left rolls or left-to-right rolls, so search out a place around a practice putting cup that affords such practice. Put down a golf tee to mark your teeing area. Use the same teeing spot for each stroke. Count the number of holed putts in ten efforts. Let your first score be your standard, or par, which you try to surpass on subsequent games of ten shots. For variation, try to hole as many putts in

This is an excellent game for developing a delicate touch on short putts. By constantly changing your target distance from 4 feet to 5 feet to 6 feet to 5 feet to 4 feet, or other variations in distance, you will smooth out your stroke and achieve great control over your ability to gauge distances and make the ball "die at the hole."

Here I am practicing long putts. I have paced off a distance of 80 feet and am using 10 balls along with my pick-up device. These balls were actually putted at the hole and were the first effort of the day. They show the common failing of all golfers, namely, coming up short of the hole.

a row as you can, forcing yourself to stop and start all over each time you miss a putt. Or see whether you can beat your previous high score on each successive group of ten putts.

Try these games for at least ten minutes of practice, possibly fifteen, depending upon your ability to maintain your concentration. Soon you will begin to achieve an automatic quality in your putting. You will begin to hole more and more putts out of ten until, finally, you may hole all ten in a row.

At that point, you probably have achieved the best results you will get on that particular putting practice day. So move your ball one foot farther away on the same line, or track, that you used previously. Continue the same practice: "how many out of ten?"

After working a while at the new distance, move another foot away from the cup. Then move back to your starting position. You may add variety to this practice technique by placing tees about an inch to each side of the cup. Then practice "sweeping" the target. Aim for the left-hand tee, then for the cup, then for the right-hand tee, then for the cup again. You simply will not believe the proficiency you can acquire if these putting practice techniques are used regularly and intelligently.

I recommend that you devote 75 percent of your putting practice to the 3-foot putt. It will pay off with generous dividends when you chip or pitch to the 3-foot distance from the hole and can follow up by sinking your putt.

The other 25 percent of your practice putting should be on longer putts, those in the 10- to 20-foot range and those in the 40- to 60-foot range. When you practice longer putts, you may want to use 10 balls

at a time instead of 5 so that you won't be bothered retrieving them so often. I like and use the tubular "Ball-Shag" for putting practice. It eliminates bending over so frequently to pick up balls.

When you practice very long putts, be sure that you are aware of the exact distance between your ball and the flagstick. Walk off the distance, counting your paces and standing carefully to the side of your putting line so that you won't ruffle it with footprints or spike marks. Since nearly all long putts are left short of the cup, make a conscious attempt to get your first long putt up to the hole.

It is very important to strike all putts squarely on the "sweet spot" of the blade, its center of gravity. If you mis-hit a putt by hitting on the toe or heel of your putter

This is called "sweeping the target." It is an excellent training method for controlling the direction of your putts. Putt alternately at the right-hand tee, the cup, the left-hand tee, the cup, and so on, back and forth, until you can hit each tee "dead on." Be sure to reassemble your stance every time or you will lose the effect of the practice. Eventually, you will find that the hole will look like a washtub to you.

Here is the three-foot-rule game. The first ball has been putted to within 6 inches of the cup and has been "penalized" 3 feet, moving it back to 3½ feet away. The other ball is at 14 inches and will be moved to 50 inches from the cup for the second effort. This game is a lot of fun and will make you realize how important it is to lay your first putt close to the hole.

blade, you will lose about 10 percent of the power normally imparted by the blade when the ball comes off the "sweet spot." On a 10-foot putt this error may amount to no more than a few inches, perhaps a foot, but on a 60-foot putt it often will be a 6-foot error; and you definitely do not want to be faced with 6-foot second putts after your long putting efforts.

When you practice long putts, it is wise, too, to attempt to duplicate conditions you will encounter on the golf course in regular play. Seek out good practice areas for fast downhill putts, slow uphill putts, and sidehill putts from all directions.

When you have someone else who will practice putting with you, you can play some interesting putting games for two. One of the best is the game of horseshoes, which is played using the same scoring as in the real game of horseshoes. Each player should play two balls, identifiable from those of his opponent. A hole-out counts three points, and the closest ball to the hole gets one or two points, depending on the positions of the other balls.

A good variation of this game is for two players to use a yardstick or a certain designated length along the putter shaft as the "penalty distance" to be applied to all putts that are not holed. It works this way: "A" putts to a distance two feet away from the target cup. "B" putts to four feet away. The distance factor is applied. "A" next putts from five feet away (two feet + three feet) on the same line to the cup. "B" putts from seven feet (four feet + three feet). You will have a much improved attitude about getting your first putt close to the hole after you have had to sink a number of six- and seven-foot putts in order to save yourself a quarter or two from a better putter than yourself!

Any putting game that makes the target smaller is a good one. Putting to a tee is good practice and makes the cup look like a washtub when you finally aim for it.

You might enjoy the "bump shot" for an unusual game. In this one, you place a golf ball on the center front edge of the cup and try to bump it in with your practice ball. If you have good overspin on your ball, it will follow the target ball into the cup. You get more points for holing both balls. Besides, you will form a more positive attitude about striking your target "dead on." You also will find that in your regular game you will aim for the center of the cup rather than for just any part of it, and you will hole many more putts than you ever did before.

I cannot overemphasize the importance of practicing your putting regularly and with a regular routine. You and I never will be able to hole every putt, but by regular, intelligent practice of a standardized putting method that obeys the fundamental rules of steady platform and smooth, repeating stroke, we will hole our share of putts and sometimes more.

It's easy to play a game of "horseshoes" on the putting green. Each player uses distinctively marked golf balls so they can be distinguished around the cup. An ace counts 3 points, and 21 points are needed to win. Here, the closest ball to the cup wins 2 points.

"Bump" may be played by one or two people. A ball is placed at the front center edge of the cup to be knocked into the hole with the putted ball. It is an excellent way to develop overspin on your putts and also is good practice at a reduced target area. If the target ball is not struck in the center, it will glance away to the side. When you can sink both balls regularly, the putted ball following the target ball into the cup, you are on your way to putting success.

Here is a view of a chip shot from
about 15 feet beyond the green to
the flagstick, which is 30 feet
downhill from the edge of the green.
This green slants to the left a little,
so I will aim about 3 feet to the right
of the flag. I am picking out the exact
spot on the green where I want my
ball to land. I see a shot traveling
one-third of its distance in the air
and running two-thirds of the way
after it has landed. A 7-iron would do
the trick, but to make sure that I
clear the longer grass on the fringe
of the green, I am using an 8-iron
and will count on less run after the
ball lands.

chapter 21

THE CHIP-AND-RUN SHOT

The language of golf is full of interesting descriptive terms. It is important that you know the proper terms for the golf shots you execute. These phrases have been in common use in golf for more than a hundred years, perhaps even longer if we had any way of eavesdropping on the golfers of Scotland in the mid-1800s.

Let us consider the "chip-and-run" shot in golf. It is executed with any club from the 4-iron down through the 8-iron. The great Arthur D. ("Bobby") Locke is said to have used nothing but his 8-iron for chips around the green. You will find that you will develop your own favorite club for the shot. Most often it is the 5-iron for the average player, particularly the beginner, probably because it gives a nice medium trajectory to the shot, not too high and not too low.

When do you use the chip-and-run shot? The first requisite is that you don't have to

contend with a bunker, long grass, or severe undulations in the green, which can interfere with your execution of the shot. It is meant to be used when the distance is just a few yards too long to putt. The idea is to "chip" the ball over rough terrain or green fringe that would interfere with and disturb the accuracy of a putt that must *roll* all the way to the hole.

The rule of thumb for this shot is to plan a one-third "chip" and two-thirds "run" to the flagstick. That is, plan to loft the ball the first third of the distance, and let it run the other two-thirds of the way to the cup. Since your overall distance will vary from shot to shot, it is clear that you must be flexible in your club selection. One time you may use your 5-iron, another time your 6, and so on. The important part of the shot is your visualization of the entire action before you make your swing. You should picture the one-third "pitch" and

This view of the chip shot on page 90 shows the ball well on its way and slightly to the right of the flagstick, where it should break to the hole after landing. Again, note my steady, unmoving head, which has not looked up although the ball has left the face of the clubhead a second or so before. Notice, too, the firm hands and wrists and the straight follow through. The clubhead only now is moving a little to the left of the target line.

This chip shot is seen from about 10 feet off the edge of the green. I am using a 5-iron. All I want to do is get the ball in the air in as low a trajectory as I can manage in order to land it on the surface of the green about 8 to 10 feet from the fringe (a good margin for error if I hit the shot too soft, since I don't want to have the ball land in the fringe and be "killed" there). I can see the precise spot where I want this shot to land, and I want it to run like a putt the rest of the way to the hole. Note the very open stance with the left foot away from the target line and the weight all on the left side of the body. Note, too, the grip is well down on the shaft for greater control.

the two-thirds "run" and see the ball accomplishing those distances in your mind's eye. It is helpful sometimes to choose a particular spot on the green where you propose to land your chip.

Some good advice in this situation is always to use a club one number higher than your first choice if there is any question in your mind as to whether or not your original choice of iron will get your ball onto the green and to the spot you have chosen. If, for example, your first survey of a chip-and-run shot leads you to believe that you will require a 6-iron to loft the ball one-third of the way to the flagstick, plan on taking the 7 instead. You then will know that you have more than enough loft, and you will be more relaxed about the shot, not worrying that it will fall short of the green, onto the fringe, and be unexpectedly "killed" there, well short of the hole. Beginner golfers consistently underestimate the loft of the pitching clubs (and many good players do the same thing in similar circumstances).

Here is a further tip on this shot and a valuable one. For a chip-and-run shot, the golfer customarily "goes down the shaft" of his club. That means that the golfer's grip moves closer to the bottom of the club, sometimes all the way down to the

metal. "Going down the shaft" gives the golfer greater control over the club, especially on the little delicate shots around the green. Finally, as you are about to address the ball, having pictured exactly where you want it to land on the green, slip your grip back up the club about one inch. Studies show that most golfers are short of the hole 90 percent of the time. This last tip, slipping the grip to a position one inch higher on the shaft, will give you more club on the ball and will help you to be up to the hole rather than short of it.

This is a front view of the proper body setup for the pitch shot. The stance is narrowed and open, that is, with the left foot drawn away from the target line. The hands are "down on the shaft" for better control of this short shot. The upper arms hug the body for a feeling of compactness and solidity.

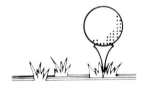

chapter 22

THE PITCH SHOT

You often will find yourself in a situation that requires you to lift the ball from its lie into the air and over some hazard or other difficulty that prevents you from getting to the hole in more normal fashion. Most often, the problem is a yawning bunker between you and the green. Or it might be anything from a small pine to a huge spreading oak tree.

This shot is called a "pitch shot" and is most often played with one of the more lofted irons, from the 7 down through the 8 and 9 to the pitching wedge or even the sand wedge. You will have to determine the angle that you want the ball to take in order to accomplish your objective. Obviously, if your ball is 60 to 70 yards from the green and the obstruction is not so high that it forces a more lofted club, you will prefer to use the 7- or 8-iron. If your ball must get up into the air quickly and also stop quickly on the green once it gets there, you will require a more lofted club, probably your pitching wedge.

The most important thought to keep in mind is the primary purpose of the shot: to get the ball up and over the obstruction or the bunker that yawns in front of you. In general, you will find that if you take "one number stronger" for this shot, you will miss it less often.

Let's consider an example of the "one number stronger" theory. You are confronted with a lie in the rough and are approximately 70 yards from the green. You have a small pine, 15 feet tall, directly in your target line and about 20 yards ahead of you. Furthermore, you have a deep trap at the green-side, also directly in front of you. Let us say that under normal conditions, that is, with no rough lie, no pine tree, and no yawning trap, just a nice open green to approach, you would use your 8-iron for the shot.

The "one number stronger" theory now comes into play. You definitely do not want to be short of the green and end up bunkered. Your lie in the rough may require more power than usual because of the added resistance from the grass behind the ball. Most important of all is the added confidence you will have when you know that you have a club strong enough to execute the shot. Thus, you select your 7-iron, the "one club stronger," and more

This view of the same pitch shot shows the one-third backswing that should be used for this type of pitch. There is some wrist break but only a slight amount, just enough to give a crisp, downward stroke through the ball. Note the steady head over the ball and the wide open stance with weight primarily on the left side of the body.

Here is a lofted pitch shot from a spot 40 yards behind the green to a flagstick that is about 30 feet downhill from the edge of the green. There is also a slope from right to left, so I have picked out the exact spot on the green where I estimate my ball should land and then drift to the left to end up near the hole. I have chosen my 9-iron because that is the club I believe will take the ball the distance I want. I had the option of using an even more lofted club, my pitching wedge, but decided that if I did, the ball might not run as far as the cup.

often than not you will accomplish the shot, carrying over the tree and bunker. In a problem situation such as this, it is frequently necessary to forget any attempt to get your ball near the flagstick. Be glad to be on the green and out of trouble.

Now let's consider the "one number stronger" theory as it applies to lofting the ball over a taller tree on your way to the green. In general, it is better to go around trees or under them rather than attempt to carry them. But every golfer will be confronted by a situation sooner or later in which he must carry over a tree or trees on his way to the green or fairway. The "one number stronger" theory works here, too.

Let us say that a first appraisal of the shot convinces you that the normal trajectory of a 5-iron will take your ball over the obstructing tree. Your lie is good, the ball is sitting up well, and you will be able to get your club on the ball easily so that the club loft will work efficiently. Again, the recommendation is to take one club

Here is the same pitch shot with the ball nicely on its way to the flag. Note the continued steady head and the distinct "hands and clubhead" follow through on the shot. On this shot keep the back of your left hand going straight at your target until the ball is well on its way. If you do this consistently, you will always be on line and need worry only about gauging the distance properly.

stronger. In this case, the "one club stronger" rule means a club with *greater* loft so that your ball will be sure to have sufficient height to carry over the tree.

To recap, the "one number stronger" theory is of utmost importance in golf strategy. You can adopt it in other ways as you progress. Some days you will find that you just are not as physically strong as on other days or as you were the last time you played golf. Often, in the early holes of a round it is well to "over-club" yourself, that is, take a slightly stronger club than you usually need for a particular shot.

Robert T. ("Bobby") Jones was famous for his golf strategy. One time, when Jones was playing a short, 3-par hole, he was asked by his playing partner at St. Andrews, "What club did you use?" Jones replied, "A mashie" (that is, a 5-iron). The opponent was surprised and said, "I hit a mashie—niblick" (meaning a 7-iron). Jones countered, "I made the green, didn't I? That's what counts!"

So, if the great Bobby Jones used the "one number stronger" rule, why shouldn't we.

This is a view from the front showing the follow through on the pitch shot, once more emphasizing the steadiness of the head over the ball and the straight follow through of the hands, arms, and clubhead down the target line. Noticeable, too, is the further turn of the lower body in its miniature swing at the ball. The weight has remained left-sided to ensure a downward stroke at the ball.

My unusual bunker practice trick, using marbles instead of golf balls. I had read of a golfer practicing with pebbles at the seashore and decided to improve on the idea. It really works to give you an exact idea of how close you are coming to hitting your target, the spot in the sand behind your ball. It also trains you to disregard the ball during the shot, an important key to success in bunker play.

chapter 23

THE SAND SHOT

Until the invention of the flange-backed sand wedge in the 1930s, getting out of sand bunkers was a very difficult problem for most golfers. It took a delicate touch, indeed, to flick the golf ball out of the sand without having the clubhead take too much sand and smother the shot. Furthermore, if the ball was the least bit buried, or "down in the sand," the shot was almost impossible.

But thanks to Gene Sarazen we have the sand wedge today, and golfers of the world now are able to extricate themselves from sand bunkers almost as easily as from deep rough. Gary Player, for example, has become so expert at getting out of sand that it is said that he often shoots for green-side bunkers rather than risk going over a green.

The sand wedge has a flange at its back that keeps the clubface from burying as the golfer strikes the sand behind his ball. It rides the sand, pushes the sand in front of it, and scoops the ball up and out toward the green. At least that is the theory of the shot. With a little practice, you can become an expert bunker player, too.

The bunker shot is one of the "illegitimate" strokes of golf in the sense that whereas the golfer frequently is admonished to "keep his eye on the ball," in the bunker shot he is told: "Forget about the ball; just keep your eye on the sand behind it." Yes, in the bunker shot the golfer does *not* hit the golf ball with the face of his club as he does in other golf strokes.

The second part of the "illegitimacy" of the sand shot lies in the altered stance of the golfer as he makes the stroke. In the bunker shot the golfer adopts a much more open stance than he uses for other golf shots. (See the photos.) The golfer's stance for the sand shot is "opened" about 20 degrees to the left of his target line, the line to the flagstick, and his swing moves along that line, 20 degrees to the left of where he really wants the shot to go. *But,* and this is

This is a close-up of a successful bunker explosion shot. The clubface is entering the sand about two and a half inches behind the ball. It appears to be farther than that, but the flange of the club creates that effect. The sand will be squeezed between the clubface and the ball, cushioning the shot. The flange will keep the club from digging too deeply into the sand and will let the clubface skim under the ball for the proper result. Note the wide-open stance, with the left foot drawn to the left while the line of flight is fifteen to twenty degrees to the right. The weight is well down on the left side and the left knee remains bent, indicating that the body is staying down until the ball is well on its way.

a most important *but,* the clubface is aligned toward the target. The result is a uniquely efficient sand-skimming by the clubface as its flanged sole enters the sand behind the ball, continues on under it, and pushes the ball up and out on a cushion of sand caught between the face of the club and the ball.

This shot should be taken with good force, the golfer exerting close to his or her maximum strength on the swing. The golfer should banish from his mind any thought of hitting the ball and concentrate on entering the sand about two or three inches behind the ball. The club is heavy and will do the work if the golfer will allow it. The golfer must "stay down" with the

shot, that is, not raise his body in the slightest until well after the ball has gone on its way out of the bunker.

The beginning golfer should make sure that his sand wedge is heavy. In my opinion, most failures to get out of bunkers occur because the golfer does not have enough help in the way of power and momentum that a heavy-headed sand wedge can supply. Once the golfer realizes that he has that power in his clubhead, he will lose his fear of bunkers and approach them confident that he can get out every time in one stroke.

Now a little advice about practicing bunker shots. With your "Ball-Shag" in hand, find a practice bunker. (I trust that your golf club, like mine, has such a thing!) Place your ball retriever about twenty-five feet from the edge of the bunker as your imaginary flagstick. Take about twenty golf balls into the bunker and spread them out in a line that runs away from you. (See photo.) For the first few shots, merely draw a line in the sand and practice entering the sand at that point until you can consistently hit your target, the line. This is to condition yourself to hit the sand and not the ball. Then start to knock a few of your golf balls out of the bunker. Find a particular grain of sand or mark about two inches behind your golf ball. Aim at it and forget about the golf ball, which merely happens to be in the way of the clubhead as it goes through the sand. Splash down through the sand, hitting your target behind the ball, and you will be amazed at the way your ball flies out of the bunker.

You will find that the correct strength of your swing coupled with the entry of the clubhead into the sand about two inches behind the ball inevitably will get the ball out of the bunker. Of course, you will make mistakes as all golfers do. You will miss your target or you will not exert enough effort in the swing. But if you practice regularly, you will learn to get out of most bunkers on the first shot.

After you have learned this basic shot, the 25-yard bunker shot, you can start to experiment with shots of various distances. By closing the blade slightly and increasing your follow through, you will be able to get another 10 to 15 yards. Later, you may experiment with hitting less sand to make the ball go even farther out of the trap. But this borders on "expert" bunker play. I suggest that for your first year or so you content yourself with getting out of bunkers with 25- to 35-yard shots in the way I have described. In the long run, you will become an expert bunker player.

Remember these fundamentals about bunker play. First, make sure your wedge is heavy enough to do the job. Second, open your stance 20 degrees to the left of your target line, but align your blade directly down that line. Swing with almost full effort through the sand, about two inches behind the ball. That will do it nine times out of ten!

Here is an example of staying down with the shot on an explosion from a bunker. Notice that my head only now is starting to move as my right shoulder, coming through the stroke, forces it up. This is another example of the tilted view the golfer should have as he sees the golf ball take off on its way to the target. Note the angle at which my head is "tilted" to the horizon and the full follow through of the hands and the clubhead.

chapter 24

THE STRATEGY OF GOLF

Golf is a "thinking person's game." Every golf course designer attempts to plan 18 holes of "challenging" golf. By that he means something like this: "I have designed this par 4 hole of 365 yards with a slight dogleg to the right and with a slight upward slope from the tee area to the green. I have put a bunker on the right front side of the green and one at the turn of the dogleg. Now let me see you play it in par!"

The "thinking golfer" looks at such a hole and at once sees the bunker ahead of him on the right-hand side. He resolves to steer clear of that obstacle if at all possible. He also will think ahead about the bunker to the right of the green and resolve to stay to the left so that his approach to the green need not be over that bunker. His eye will see the up-slope toward the green, and his mind will register the need for "more club," that is, a stronger club, to carry all the way to an elevated green. With all of these factors in mind, not to mention such things as wind direction and condition of course (hard and fast, soft and slow, for example), he is ready to play the hole intelligently.

Certainly, things may go wrong, but when they do not, the golfer not only has the physical satisfaction of playing the hole well but also the mental satisfaction of "solving the hole," beating the architect at his own game.

As you play golf on your "home" course (for most golfers seem to confine their play to one or possibly two courses), you should analyze constantly, hole-by-hole, how you think the architect meant you to play each hole. You will get to know your capabilities and faults, your strong points and your weak points. Let us say that you are reconciled to the fact that you are not and never will be a long driver in golf. Your longest drive is, say, in the 180-yard range. With

an acceptance of your golfing fate, your strategy in playing long par 4 holes and longer par 5 holes, too, must be built upon the actualities of your driving game. You will attempt to avoid bunkers at the 170- to 180-yard range, and you will work hard to improve your pitching and chipping game from 50 yards away from the flag. You will reconcile yourself to the fact that you just won't be able to reach distant greens in "regulation figures," that is, one stroke to a 3-par, two strokes to a 4-par, and three strokes to a 5-par.

But, on the other hand, you will take pleasure in golf anyway because you will occasionally or even frequently get your par by a good chip and putt or a good pitch and putt. Always remember the wonderful and sound golf adage attributed to Tom Sayers: "The man who can putt can play anybody." That can be expanded to, "The man who can chip and putt can play anybody." And both adages are perfectly true.

Let's talk a little more about the strategy of golf. Presuming that like all beginner golfers (as well as nearly all golfers, beginners or veterans) you dread a golf shot that must carry a water hazard, a ditch, or a lake, your strategy certainly is going to be to steer clear of them. But there are certain times when the golfer is confronted with that terrifying water hazard and must face it, hoping to conquer it straightaway. There is no escape route. Your strategy from the tee might be to plan for the confrontation with the hazard.

A golfer's fear of water often is based upon the usually irrevocable loss of his ball in the hazard. So accept the possible loss of the ball, but let the lost ball be one of your oldest "duds," not a nice new one. Carry a supply of old balls with you so that when you are faced with a situation that may cost you a ball, whether in a water hazard or out-of-bounds in some wilderness, you will not worry about the loss. (A golfer is permitted to change balls any time the ball has suffered damage, or he may begin any hole with a new or different ball.) Oddly, when you are prepared for such an eventuality, you will find that you are more relaxed and often will execute a most satisfactory shot that ends up on the fairway or the green.

Your strategy necessarily must be based upon the actualities of your golf game, your strengths and weaknesses. And that is one of the reasons why you will find considerable emphasis in this book on practice, both on a golf range and in the privacy of your own home. You will soon come to realize your weaknesses in golf, and by constant practice on each particular weakness, you will improve your "batting average," your percentage of satisfactory shots contrasted with your percentage of bad shots.

Walter Hagen, one of the greatest golfers of all time, used to say: "I'm going to make at least three mistakes on each round. So when I make the first one I am not upset. It was one of those I was going to make anyway." With this attitude of accepting errors as inevitable and trying constantly to improve every phase of the golf game, there is no question but that the beginner will succeed in becoming a true golfer and, what's more, will find great enjoyment in the game!

Tee-shot strategy is a most important part of the game. Here I have teed my ball on the right-hand side of the tee area in order to play away from that large bush on the right. There is also a bunker ahead on the right-hand side at the 200-yard mark of this hole, and I want to stay away from it, too.

chapter **25**

STRATEGY OF THE TEE-SHOT

Many golfers are careless about teeing up their tee-shots. If you will pay particular attention to a number of foursomes proceeding, one after the other, from the first tee of any golf course, you will notice how few of the golfers really look the teeing ground over for unevenness and search out the best possible teeing area. On the other hand, if you will observe any one of the great professional golfers appearing in nationally televised golf tournaments, you will notice that each is most careful about where he tees his golf ball. Sometimes you will even see a professional who has already teed-up change his mind and re-tee his ball in another place.

Start out with a professional's wisdom about playing your tee-shot. Don't ever count on a golf tee being level! From my long experience in golf, I believe it is safe to say that with the exception of certain golf courses that are maintained in impeccable condition, most golf course tees have

some areas that are level and some areas that are *not* level. Once in a while you will find a tee that has *no* level spot, and then you must do your best with a bad situation, adopt a sidehill or downhill stance, and execute the shot in the best way you can.

Here is the procedure that the professionals go through in selecting the best teeing area for themselves. You can and should use it, too. First, be aware that while it is true that you must tee off in an area that lies between the tee-markers, you have the further option of teeing your ball anywhere in that rectangular plot of turf that lies parallel to the markers to a distance of two club lengths behind them. (An accompanying photo shows the teeing area available on the first hole at Atlantis Golf Club, my home course.) Your position may even be outside the teeing area as long as the ball itself is inside of it. In determining where to tee your ball, first step

Looking for a level place before taking your stance on the tee. Be aware that you are entitled to use the area two club lengths behind the markers and that you may even stand outside the teeing area as long as the ball itself is struck from within it.

four or five paces behind the teeing area and look over the terrain between the markers for levelness and for depressions from old divot marks left by other golfers. You should be able to see or sense in the soles of your feet whether or not the terrain is level, from the front of the tee to the back or if there is a slope up or down.

Next, search out the most level area for both the ball and your stance. There may be several places that are suitable. Consider each one as you mentally determine your tee-shot strategy for the hole. There may be a number of reasons for teeing your ball on one side of the tee or the other. The presence of a tree or bunker on one side of the fairway may tell you to favor the side of the tee that will let you aim away from the hazard, for, in general, it is best to tee-up on the side of the tee nearest the hazard and play away from it.

Tee your ball to normal height under most conditions of golf. (See Chapter 33 for exceptions.) Assume your stance and make sure you feel at ease. If you find that you do not have your usual sense of balance, coming up from your swing platform, in the soles of your feet and in your legs, stop right there and walk away from the shot. In nearly every case where this happens, the golfer unknowingly has placed one foot or the other in an old divot mark, which is affecting his ability to "get set" for his shot. You are under no obligation to play from an unsuitable teeing place. You will botch the shot if you do, probably because your swing will not be "normal." Step away and re-tee your ball in another place that does allow you good balance.

As I already have pointed out, it is possible that there will be no truly level place for your tee-shot. When this happens, and it will, you must accept it as part of the fortunes of golf and work with it.

Let us presume that the teeing area is off-level with the golfer's feet below the ball no matter where he tees it. Be aware of this, by all means, and plan to execute a shot that takes into consideration the inescapable fact that your feet are below the ball. Most right-handed golfers will hook, or pull to the left of their intended line, when their feet are lower than the ball. Therefore, in this situation the golfer should adjust his aiming point to the right of his normal line, possibly even toward the right-hand rough, and proceed to drive. Very likely you will pull the ball into the fairway for a satisfactory result.

A further tip on tee-shot strategy: Be careful to avoid overhanging trees and tree branches by teeing your ball on one side of the tee area or another. Visualize the intended path of your shot, and if there is even a remote possibility that a tree will interfere with it, adjust your strategy accordingly. Shoot away from it as much as you can, just as you would avoid a bunker at the edge of the fairway.

If you pay special attention to your teeing spot on every tee, you will save from one to two strokes in each round of golf. Furthermore, you will gain a great deal of personal satisfaction when you see an opponent drive into an overhanging tree that you carefully and successfully avoided. Golf is a thinking person's game. Be sure to think on every tee!

Here is the great "Ball-Shag" device that will handle comfortably about forty golf balls. When I use it for bunker practice, as I am doing here, I place the device on the green to act as my imaginary flagstick. Whenever you practice, you should always have a target in mind.

chapter 26

HOW TO PRACTICE GOLF

In my lifetime of golf I always have been an avid practicer of the game. I recommend that you, too, consider practice not as a chore or a burdensome duty but as the pleasure and fun it can be when it is carried out intelligently.

One of the unpleasant phases of practicing golf has been the necessity of leaning over constantly to pick up golf balls. This problem now has been solved. In the 1940s came the invention of the "Ball-Shag," which is illustrated in the pictures. This handy device comes in two different models. I suggest that you order both from your local golf supply store.

The larger model is meant to be used by the serious practicer and will hold about fifty golf balls comfortably. The smaller tube model will hold about twenty-five balls. The bottom of the tube has some ingenious metal "fingers" that slip over the ball and pick it up. Successive pickups push the balls up the tube. The tube model will fit easily into your golf bag so that wherever you go you can carry your supply of practice balls.

As you play golf, you will find that golf balls damage easily. You will mis-hit a ball and discover that it now has a damaged cover. Or a ball will be scratched or marred as it bounces off a cart path or a tree trunk. I suggest that you accept these occurrences as part of the luck of the game, retire the ball from competition, and put it into your practice bag. You will end up with excellent, usable practice balls, much better than the ones you might rent to practice at your nearby driving range. Driving ranges must plan to get a lot of mileage from their golf balls, so they often use very hard, solid balls, which do give a lot of use but are very unpleasant to strike. We will talk about the use of the solid ball in your own game a little later.

Another item I suggest you use in practice sessions is an old white bath towel for a target. I have made my own target from an old, worn-out bed sheet. It is cut into a circular shape with a seven- or eight-foot diameter, and it can be carried easily in the side pocket of my golf bag.

Let's say that I want to practice pitches at a 75-yard distance. I take my "Ball-Shag" to the practice area I prefer, alongside the practice range of my own golf club, dump the 50 balls, and then walk out 75 paces to place my "target." While my stride is a little less than 36 inches, I still practice at what are, in my own mind, 75 Taylor "yards." The correction is minor, perhaps a foot or two. I anchor the target

with a few tees around its edge and then put my red "Ball-Shag" in the center to represent the flagstick at which I will be aiming.

Now I am ready for some serious 75-yard practice. I will hit 2 or 3 "sets" of 20 or 25 balls to the target. I retrieve each group of balls after I have hit them because I have found that my concentration seems to wander after I have hit that many balls in succession. My mind will be recording how close I am coming to the target and also how many bad shots I have hit out of the number I have made. Particularly, I will be paying attention to the real-

This is pitching practice to my target and my imaginary flagstick, the red "Ball-Shag" device. I know that this pitch is exactly 40 yards long, and I will count how many balls out of ten I get on my target. Note the follow through of the clubhead toward the target. It proves that the back of my left hand was heading directly for the target at the moment of impact with the ball.

Another view of practicing pitch shots. Notice the extremely "open" stance with nearly all the weight on the left side of the body. Steadiness of the head and body is apparent during the shot; do not look up to see where the ball has gone.

More pitching practice. I cannot emphasize too strongly the necessity for you to "stay with the shot," that is, keep your head steady during the swing and "down" at impact as you pitch or chip. It is sound advice for any shot but crucial to success in the short shots. Although the ball is nicely on its way to the target, my head has not "come up" at all. I recommend keeping your head down for at least ten successive shots without raising it between shots. It's an idea I got from Gary Player when I watched him practice at Oakland Hills for an Open championship. It has paid off with great dividends over the years.

ly wild shots, the ones that fall very short or a great distance off-line. I am attempting to get into my mind my "percentage of perfection." If I can hit 20 out of 25 good shots, I feel that I have attained a certain level of perfection. And I keep that percentage in mind so that when I am in a formal game and am confronted with the same kind of shot, I will know that my chances are 20 out of 25 of coming fairly close to my target. In that way, my mind is prepared for the occasional bad shot. I calm myself by saying that the bad shot is only 1 of those 5 out of 25 that would have gone wrong anyway.

You will find, as I have over the years, that your percentage of perfection will vary from day to day, from week to week, from year to year. Some days you will be able to hit nearly every shot well and come near your target with great frequency. On other days it will be just the reverse. Nothing seems to go right. You miss many shots. Don't worry when this happens to you; it happens to all golfers. You must accept the changes that occur in your game, your swing, your physical makeup from day to day. In the long run everything will even out, and you will achieve a level of perfection, a certain "handicap" in the game, at which you will play consistently.

As my practice session ends, I will either move the target another 10 yards away or I will move backward on my practice tee the same distance. This gives me a sharper ability to discriminate between the 75-yard shot and the 85-yard shot. You will find that the more you practice varying the distance, the more you truly will achieve. You will need to strike the ball just a bit harder to make it go the extra 10 yards. And, most pleasantly, you will discover that your mind is registering that fact, your muscles are obeying, and the ball is going that slight distance farther. At

first you may find that you overshoot the longer target by quite a distance. But as you continue to work, you will be able to hit the 85-yard target just as easily and as accurately as you did the 75-yard target.

Although I suggest that you use the 75-yard practice distance, there is no reason why you cannot use any distance you wish. It might be 25 yards at the start. Then lengthen it to 35 yards and then to 50. The important thing is to understand what you are trying to do: hit a golf ball consistently a certain, predetermined distance and in the direction you choose.

You can vary this practice by trying to loft your ball all the way to your target, as if you were trying to hole out a 75-yard shot on the fly. Then on the next shot try to strike the ball so that it lands in front of your target and bounces onto the target area. This is another method of gaining what is called a discriminating touch in golf.

The longer clubs are a little more difficult to practice with when you are alone. Ideally, you will want to find a practice area that is unobstructed and has enough length so that you can "spray" a few shots, as you undoubtedly will. If there are other golfers practicing nearby, you will run into the annoying problem of separating your own practice balls from those of the other golfers. When this happens, my recommendation is that you stop practicing entirely because you will not be able to concentrate on your own game when you are worried about losing your practice balls. Go to the driving range, use their balls even though they are not as pleasant to hit as your own, and fire away without worrying about losing the practice balls. That's the range-owner's worry!

You must always practice with a target in mind and in view. If you are working on direction alone, you might decide not to worry about distance and just concentrate on hitting the ball in the desired direction. But, on the whole, always look for a target and attempt to hit that target. On a driving range it might be a tree in the distance, a certain discolored spot in the fairway, a particular golf ball that is lying on the range. It might be a caddie shagging for you, although most beginner golfers find that using a caddie to shag balls is distracting. For some perverse reason, when the caddie is there as a target, there is pressure on the golfer to hit the ball straight at him. And with that pressure comes an inability to do so. My suggestion is that you do your own shagging, as I do with the ball "picker-upper." It is a much more relaxing method of practice.

You will encounter good lies, fair lies, bad lies, and "impossible" lies in your golf career. Therefore, it is wise to prepare for every situation. In my opinion, you should emphasize practice on the more difficult shots rather than on the easier ones. I will concede that the beginner should learn first how to hit the ball from a tee or from a good lie on the practice tee, with the ball "sitting up" fairly on splendid terrain.

But once the beginner golfer has learned to strike the ball consistently from good lies, he should start to practice more difficult shots than easy ones. So, early on, begin to hit the ball out of fair lies, where the ball is on rather closely cropped grass, and then out of decidedly bad lies, where the ball is down in the grass or in a cuppy lie. It is wise, too, to practice out of both light rough and heavy rough. The distinction between the two kinds of rough will become evident to you the more you play golf on different courses. In general, light rough has grass cut to about a two-inch height while heavy rough is allowed to grow much longer and may not be cut at all on some courses.

When you practice the difficult shots, you are strengthening your game so that you will face practically no golf problem that you have not experienced before and, thus, will have some idea for a solution.

Try to become familiar with winds from all directions. Look forward to a strong wind that presents a challenge on the practice tee. Practice from one end of the tee toward the other end, and then reverse your field in order to experience the wind from exactly the opposite direction. Remember that many golf courses are built so that the situation exactly opposite from that of lying in deep rough is a bare lie, or what is sometimes called "hardpan." Golf courses do not water their rough as assiduously as they do their fairways and greens. The result is that the ground in rough areas often will become baked hard from the summer sun and lack of water. The grass will be sparse or nonexistent or will grow in tufts with small dry craters between the tufts. Your ball will come to rest on what seems to be concrete, or it will nestle into one of the shallow craters.

These trouble shots are difficult for even the best players, so don't be disappointed if you have difficulty with them, too. The only way to execute these shots is to hit the ball first in your downswing, that is, do not allow the clubhead to touch the ground before the clubface gets to the ball. Hit the ball cleanly, with the blade continuing down through the shot. And if you don't succeed, don't worry about it. It takes a true expert to make such a precise shot, but knowing what to do is half the battle.

In practice sessions, I have emphasized the importance of learning how to hit the ball out of all kinds of lies and from various uneven terrains. Now your practice will pay off. Concentrate on making the best possible swing at the ball. Do not think, "I must get this ball up and out of

Here is Horton Smith with the practice swing device called the "Swing-Rite." It has a weight that clicks at the point of maximum acceleration in the swing. If the golfer does not achieve his highest rate of acceleration at the point of impact, the absence of the "click" promptly tells him so. Horton believed this device was very useful for beginner golfers by giving them a clear understanding of the importance of swing acceleration.

this tight lie," a thought that might cause you to dig at the ball or scrape at it instead of making a good swing. Think "swing"— and there is a good possibility for success.

Here is a list of some of the many practice devices you may buy and use:

Any of the putting practice mechanisms, especially the ones that will return the putted ball to you.

Putting cups that have hinged gates to trap the golf ball.

Putting carpets with inclines and real putting cups.

Brass clips that fit on your putter head and force you to strike the putt on the sweet spot of the club.

Weighted golf clubs with shortened grips and added weight at their tips.

The "Warm-Up" weighted head cover that fits over your wood clubhead and increases its weight to about 24 ounces.

"The Grip," a molded golf club grip that has indentations to fit your fingers and force you to assume a correct grip.

The "Swing-Rite," a shortened golf club engineered to give a sharp "click" as the golfer attains maximum clubhead speed in the hitting area but will not "click" if the momentum does not occur at the proper part of the swing. This is a very good trainer to stop "hitting from the top" of the swing.

Films and filmstrips of great golfers also are available and are of great instructional value. The newest and best have just been announced and marketed by golf enthusiast James Quinn. You may obtain three-dimensional filmstrips of Lee Trevino and others in action.

If you are interested in seeing motion pictures of some of the greatest golf courses in the world, write to Shell Oil Company for films of their television series "Wonderful World of Golf," which was made all over the world and stars great golfers in head-to-head matches. The U.S.G.A. also has an extensive library with many historic teaching films available on request to established golf groups. The Cadillac Motor Division of General Motors has many films of the Master's Tournaments played at the famous Augusta National Golf Club. These are especially worth viewing for their scenic beauty as well as for glimpses of many foreign star golfers.

chapter 27

RULES, ETIQUETTE, AND ADAGES OF GOLF

THE RULES OF GOLF

The United States Golf Association determines the rules of golf for golfers in the United States. It acts in conjunction with the Royal and Ancient Golf Club of St. Andrews, Scotland, which is the supreme arbiter of golf rules around the world. The American golfer plays a slightly larger golf ball than does the overseas player. The variance is small, only a few hundredths of an inch in diameter, 2.68 vs. 2.65 inches, but the smaller ball is decidedly easier to handle in the strong winds that prevail in Scotland, Ireland, and England. The use of the smaller English ball is illegal in America. You might be tempted to try it out sometime in an American wind. I urge you to do so for your own amazement at how differently the ball handles not only in the wind but in liveliness around the greens in chip-and-run shots. But don't play the ball in American competition, even in your

"friendly foursome," as it is considered cheating to do so.

It is most important that you learn the rules of golf. You do not need to memorize them, but certain important ones about your rights and obligations concerning a lost ball, a ball out-of-bounds, or a ball in a water hazard are most important to know because those predicaments occur with regularity as you play. Not knowing how to proceed under the rules may give you basic insecurity about your game and cause embarrassment as you play golf.

A complete book, *Rules of Golf,* usually is available at your nearest professional's golf shop. If you have any difficulty finding it, you may write to the United States Golf Association, Golf House, Far Hills, New Jersey 07931, and they will gladly arrange to send it to you for a small fee.

I recommend that you read the rules,

study the most difficult or complicated situations, and, as you encounter various problems with the interpretation of the rules as you play, do not be afraid or ashamed to ask more experienced players their opinions as to how the rules apply. Always keep in mind that in cases of doubt a second ball, or "provisional ball," can be played, with both balls holed out independently and the final score held in abeyance until an official interpretation of the rules can be made.

By no means turn into "a walking rule book," as some players are apt to do, calling each and every minor infraction of the rules on another player. It is up to the player himself to call most violations, for example, when he suffers an out-of-bounds penalty or his ball moves off its axis after he has addressed it. In the case of a questionable call as to whether or not a ball lies out-of-bounds, it is polite to ask your partner or opponent to help you sight along the line between the two nearest white stakes to determine if the ball lies outside or inside the imaginary line. Remember, if any part of the ball is touching the line, it is considered in-bounds.

Only the most flagrant violation of the rules should be enforced against another player. This, too, can be done in a polite, tactful manner. The most frequent abuse, in my opinion, is reporting, intentionally or unintentionally, a lower score than that actually made by the player.

This situation can be remedied politely and quickly if it is done in the following manner. The player who suspects another of under-counting his score, counts the strokes mentally as the opponent plays the hole. After three or four strokes, he says something such as, "Let's see, I lie three and you lie four." Note that he does not end with the question, "Don't you?" He *tells* the other player what he lies. The other player soon gets the message and

either desists or is caught redhanded by the watchful player when the scores are reported upon completion of the hole. The dialogue might go something like this after a player has reported a seven that should have been an eight: "Let's see, you were in the rough in two, one into the fairway for three, fourth into the bunker, and five on the green. Didn't you take three putts? I think you had eight. Well, you count them again because I might be wrong."

You may obtain a small folder entitled "Golf Rules in Brief" from the U.S.G.A. This is a handy reference that explains the most important rules in golf and pays particular attention to those rules the golfer is most apt to encounter in an ordinary round. You should plan to carry "Golf Rules in Brief" in your golf bag so that you can refer to it if necessary. It is advisable, too, to carry the complete book of rules in your bag, although it is not indexed very well and you may find it difficult to extract the precise ruling you need from a plethora of rules about sizes and shapes of golf equipment and other abstruse subjects.

Here is a summary of the rules of golf for you to read and study until you obtain your own copies of "Golf Rules in Brief" and the complete *Rules of Golf*. Since changes in the rules occur frequently, you should try to stay up-to-date with the latest official rules of golf at all times.

Starting to Play Golf

1. Play only the American-size golf ball.
2. You may carry no more than 14 clubs.
3. Be sure to tee your ball between the tee-markers and in the rectangle that extends from the front of the markers to two club-lengths behind the markers.
4. The player who won the last hole has the "honor" and plays first from the next tee.
5. The player whose ball is farthest from

the hole plays his ball first.

6. You must hit the ball with your club-head, not push it or scrape it.
7. You may take advice from your caddie or your partner, no one else.
8. You are not allowed to use any "trick" measuring devices to gauge distances.
9. Do not delay your play or the play of others.

(Rules 2, 3, 9, 12, 13, 19, 20, and 27)

Play of the Ball

1. Play the ball where it lies no matter how "badly" it lies. This rule is the heart of the game, and obedience to it is the sign of a true golfer.
2. If your ball becomes damaged in any way, you may replace it with another without penalty.
3. Be careful to play your own ball. If you play the wrong ball, you suffer a one-stroke penalty in medal play, loss of the hole in match play.

(Rules 16, 21, and 28)

Rules About the Course

1. Play the course as you find it.
2. There is no difference between fairway and rough as far as the rules are concerned. A "hazard" is either a bunker (sand or grass trap) or water.
3. You are not allowed to move, bend, or break anything fixed or growing except in "fairly taking your stance" or making your swing. Don't press down on the turf behind your ball or do anything else that will aid your stroke.
4. When you are in a hazard, you may not "ground" your club, that is, touch the ground, the sand, or the water before your downswing.
5. If your ball comes to rest on the wrong putting green, you may drop off without penalty.

Loose Impediments

1. Stones and leaves are considered loose impediments, and you may remove them unless you encounter them in a hazard. Then, you may not.
2. If your ball moves "off its axis" and fails to return to its original place, you suffer a one-stroke penalty. There is no penalty, though, if this happens on the putting green.

(Rules 18 and 35)

Obstructions

1. Basically, if an obstruction has been made by man, you are allowed "relief" from it. If it is movable, you can move it without penalty. If you cannot move it (a bridge, for example), you may drop your ball two club-lengths away from it without penalty.

(Rule 31)

If Your Ball Moves Accidentally

1. If your ball is moved accidentally by you, your partner, or by one of your caddies (usually by stepping on it), you play it where it lies and add a penalty stroke.
2. If someone else or something else, a dog, for instance, moves it, replace it where it was without penalty.

(Rule 27)

Lost Ball, Unplayable Ball, Out-of-Bounds

1. When you lose your ball or knock it out-of-bounds, you must replay the stroke from where you hit it and add a stroke penalty. If you were on the tee, you may re-tee the ball.
2. If your ball is unplayable, you may treat it the same way as you would a lost ball, or you may drop the ball at least two club-lengths, not nearer the

hole, behind the unplayable spot and add one penalty stroke. If you are in a bunker, you must re-drop in the bunker.

(Rule 29)

Ball in Water Hazard

1. You may drop either behind the hazard or at the place where you played your last stroke and add one penalty stroke.
2. If you are in a "lateral" water hazard, you have the additional option of dropping within two club-lengths of the hazard on either side of it and opposite the spot where the ball entered the hazard and add one penalty stroke.

(Rule 33)

Provisional Ball

1. You are allowed to play a provisional ball if you believe your original ball may be lost or out-of-bounds. You should play the provisional ball before you proceed to look for the original ball. Tell your partner and opponents, "I'm going to play a provisional ball."

(Rule 30)

Casual Water, Ground Under Repair, Holes Made by Burrowing Animals

1. If you find your ball in casual water (if you can see water expressed from the ground as you step on it), you are in casual water and may drop away from it without penalty. If you are in "G.U.R.," "Ground Under Repair" (the area must be marked as such to qualify) or in an animal's burrowing hole, you may drop as near as possible or within two club-lengths, not nearer the hole, to the original lie on the putting green or in a hazard.

(Rule 32)

The Proper Procedure for Dropping a Ball

1. When you are permitted a "drop" under the rules, stand facing the hole and drop the ball over your shoulder.
2. If the ball ends up nearer the hole, more than two club-lengths away, goes out-of-bounds or into a hazard, or strikes you before it hits the ground, you must drop it again.
3. If you are allowed a drop in a hazard, the dropped ball must remain in the hazard after the drop.

(Rule 22)

The Putting Green

1. You may not touch your putting line unless you are permitted to do so under the rules. For example, you may scrape away a worm cast or remove a loose piece of gravel.
2. You may not test the surface of the green by scraping it or rolling a ball on it.
3. You are entitled to lift and clean your ball on the putting green, not on the apron or fringe of the green. Replace it on the same spot.
4. You may repair a ball divot mark on the green but may not repair spike marks raised by golf shoes. (Note: This rule may be changed in the near future, in my opinion.)
5. No one but your caddie or partner is allowed to point out the line of your putt.
6. If another ball is in your path to the cup, you may ask to have it marked and lifted. If your ball, played from the putting green, hits another ball, you suffer a two-stroke penalty in medal play but no penalty in match play.
7. Always hole out your ball or you will be deemed not to have completed the hole.

Your opponent in a match may concede your putt. Then you are considered to have holed in the next stroke.

8. If your ball hangs on the very edge of the hole, you are allowed to wait only a few seconds to determine whether it is at rest or not.

(Rule 35)

The Flagstick

1. If your ball strikes the flagstick when played from the putting green, you suffer a two-stroke penalty in medal play, and you lose the hole in match play.

(Rule 34)

The Application of the Rules

1. Many golf courses have local rules that are not incorporated into the general rules of golf and, in some cases, supersede them. Be sure to read each golf course's scorecard and note any local rule that affects your play.

2. If there is any question on the interpretation of a rule of golf, the golf committee at the golf course makes the final decision.

3. You may not agree to ignore the rules or waive penalties. If you do, you are subject to disqualification.

(Rules 4, 11, and 36)

THE ETIQUETTE OF GOLF

Golf is a "gentleman's game" played by gentlemen and, of course, gentlewomen! There is a quaint set of standards that have governed the etiquette of golf for centuries. Knowing them and practicing them will add to your knowledge and enjoyment of the game, will mark you as an "insider," one who knows golf and is, therefore, a gentleman or gentlewoman golfer.

One of the most important aspects of golf etiquette deals with your attitude toward your own game and toward that of your opponent. The *Rules of Golf,* which governs the play and conduct of golfers all over the world, does not, in many cases, spell out the finer nuances of politeness that are observed by "true golfers."

For example, unlike other sports, the golfer never "needles" his opponent in an attempt to upset his game. Much as you might hope for a badly played shot by your opponent, you never make a comment to that effect. On the other hand, you should compliment him on his best shots and even on some shots that border on the mediocre.

Always be observant of your opponent's playing situation, and be careful not to interfere in any way with his ability to make his next shot. This means that you stand still and do not make noise or movements that might distract his concentration. In golf the player farthest from the flagstick is said to be "away" and is the player who takes the next shot.

If there is any doubt as to whether your ball or your opponent's ball is farthest from the hole, ask politely, "Am I away or are you?" before proceeding. If it appears that both balls are equidistant from the hole, it is polite to defer to your opponent by saying: "If you're ready, make your shot." At any rate, do not make a "federal case" out of the matter. Proceed with the play expeditiously.

It also follows that you should play the game as quickly and yet as comfortably as possible. It is unnecessary for a golfer to take repeated practice strokes before his real one or to delay a long time while selecting a club. Although the rules of golf allow a few minutes search for a golf ball, rarely does the true golfer take advantage of this rule and prolong a search for an obviously lost ball. He declares it "lost" quickly and gets on with the game.

Politeness also requires that a golfer help find the lost ball of anyone in his foursome. Don't wait to do this, either, as an extra pair of eyes looking for a ball in deep rough often will make the difference between finding and losing the ball.

You should familiarize yourself with the rules of golf concerning lost balls, especially with your right to play a provisional ball under circumstances that would lead you to believe your ball might either be lost or out-of-bounds. It is a very useful rule and helps to speed up play in the event the ball does turn out to have been lost.

Politeness enters the game in the lost ball situation, too. The true golfer is always aware that he may be delaying players behind him on the course, and as soon as there is a delay, such as looking for a lost ball or excessively slow play, he immediately "waves on" the group behind him and allows them to "go through" as a matter of right rather than as a favor granted.

On the putting green, a great deal of golf etiquette is practiced. By knowing and understanding it you will become a more knowledgeable and accepted golfer. Be careful that you do not step on the line your opponent's ball will take to the hole. Especially on wet greens, a golfer's footprints will leave a slight impression, enough to cause a serious variation in the normally smooth track of the ball to the hole.

It often will happen that your ball is near or on your opponent's intended putting line to the hole. You should be prepared to mark your own ball in a careful fashion in accordance with the rules of golf. Carefully place a quarter or dime under and directly behind your ball. Remove the ball. Under present rules, you may wipe and clean your ball while it is so marked. Let your opponent putt his stroke

to the hole. Then replace your ball, as carefully as you marked it, on exactly the same spot on the green.

Occasionally, the marker of a marked ball will remain in the line of a putt. It is polite then to move your marker one or two clubhead-lengths out of the line. Once more, I suggest that you do this with mathematical precision. Watch the professionals in their televised golf tournaments and see how they do it. They will sight a target such as a nearby tree and, having carefully set their putters at a right angle to that target, will move their ball markers a clubhead-length away to one side or the other. In replacing the ball, they will go through the same procedure: sight the target, measure the clubhead-length again, and replace the ball on its spot.

When a member of your foursome apparently has lost his ball, it is a custom of the game that the other members help him find it. Obviously, four pairs of eyes are more likely to discover it in heavy rough than only one pair. You will find, too, that if you are vigilant and consistently watch the tee-shots (and other shots, too) of your fellow players, you can act as a watchdog and thus save some time while playing golf.

There is a trick to marking the position of a possibly lost ball. Once you learn it and use it, you will be able to find golf balls more easily than other players who do not understand the principle. The trick is to position yourself so that you are in line with the shot and thus able to keep your eye on the ball as long as possible while it is in flight. When it disappears into woods or heavy rough, raise your eyes and "mark" some tree, bush, or other distinctive ground feature nearby as a reference point. When you proceed toward the ball, do not deviate from the line toward that marked object. Walk straight toward it, and your chances are good that the ball will lie within a few yards to one side or the other of the line. Make it a habit not only to watch your own ball but also to be alert to what happens to the drives of your fellow players. You will be surprised to find that many players have no idea where a lost golf ball might be because they fail to use this "lining up" technique. You will save your own time and find many a "lost ball" if you locate it ahead of time in the manner suggested.

Another interesting and useful technique you can and should use to aid your partner or opponent consists of making yourself a "human semaphore" when the target green or flagstick is out of a player's field of vision. Let us presume that one player is down the side of a hill and cannot see the green from his position. The other player should go to the top of the hill and maneuver himself until one of his arms is pointing to the green and the other directly at the player. The player then can mark some discoloration or shrub on the terrain as in line with the green, and the "human semaphore" can move out of the way. In these circumstances, too, it is polite for the player who has indicated the direction of the shot to remain to one side and watch the flight of the ball for the other player who cannot follow it himself.

The rules of etiquette that apply in golf are, for the most part, based upon the etiquette of everyday life and common politeness to others. Probably the most important rule of etiquette deals with speed of play. No one should delay the play of a golf stroke unnecessarily. It disregards the interests of others when a player delays in choosing his club or, when looking for a lost ball, fails to "wave on" following players. It also is only common courtesy to finish a hole promptly as soon as the last putt is sunk. The scorecard is never marked while the scorekeeper is still on the green, only after the green has been cleared for the next players.

Golf etiquette requires, too, that no one intentionally or unintentionally distracts another player while he is preparing to make his stroke or executing it. No one should move, talk, or stand close to or directly behind either the ball or the hole when a player is addressing the ball or making a stroke.

The courteous golfer always smooths out the marks he has left in a sand bunker as a result of his shot, his stance, and his footprints. He also carefully replaces his divots and tamps them down so that they have a chance to grow again.

You should know the etiquette of handling the flagstick for another golfer. If a golfer has put his ball on a green but at a substantial distance from the hole, he may want the flagstick left in the hole so that he can "see the hole" more clearly. But, under the rules of golf, once his ball has reached the green, the golfer must not strike the flagstick for fear of incurring a penalty shot. (See *Rule 34-3:* "The player's ball shall not strike the flagstick in the hole unattended when the ball has been played from the putting green.")

Therefore, either a caddie, one of the playing partners, or an opponent "attends the flag" for the putter. The attendant stands beside the flagstick with his hand on the pole ready to remove the flagstick once the putt is struck and on its way to the hole. The proper way to perform the act of "attending the flag" is to face the golfer who is putting and stand at a right angle to the line of the putt in such a position that the shadow of the person holding the pole does not cross the line of the putt. There is an odd jinx in golf about putting through a shadow, so you must be careful not to let your shadow fall on the putting line.

Another good tip for the one attending the flag is to make sure that the flagstick can be removed easily from the cup when you want to take it out. Sometimes the bottom of the flagstick will wedge itself into the socket of the cup, and when the person attending the flagstick tugs on the pole, instead of coming out of the hole properly, the pole sticks in its socket, and to everyone's surprise, especially the one attending the flag, the liner of the cup comes out with the flagstick and raises its edge above the cut edge of the hole. If the golfer putting happens to strike the metal cup liner with his putt, his ball might ricochet a substantial distance away from the hole and, of course, he misses the shot.

It is polite, too, to inquire whether or not a fellow player wants the flagstick attended. Phrase your request this way: "Do you want me to take the flagstick for you or would you rather have it left?" I have observed golfers who consistently want the flagstick attended up to distances of only ten or fifteen feet from the hole. On the other hand, some golfers want the pole out even on chips from off the green, where they have a perfect right to leave the pole in. You will find that it is sometimes wise to leave the flagstick in when your chipshot is coming from above the hole on a fast, slippery green. The pole may act as a backstop for your ball, and you might hole a shot that you otherwise would not.

THE ADAGES AND SUPERSTITIONS OF GOLF

There are many adages in golf, some that have become clichés over the years. However, you should know them because they are part of the lore of golf. The most famous is "never up, never in," which refers to the putt that falls short of the cup. Another is the term "gimmie," which is the question a player will ask when he would like to have a short putt conceded to him. It is used in two ways: "Will you give me [gimmie] that putt?" or, "Is this a gim-

mie?" meaning is this putt short enough so that you think I won't miss it.

You should never resort to begging for a putt to be conceded to you nor should you consider yourself a bad sport when you refuse to concede a short putt to an opponent. The request usually connotes a fear that you might miss the putt. You may refuse to concede a short putt by saying in a mock-serious manner, "No, but I would if it were one inch shorter" or, "No, I'd rather watch your beautiful, smooth putting stroke while you make it."

Another, lesser known adage is "three up with five to play never wins." This refers to match play, and in many cases the adage does prove true. The player with a large margin late in the match often will falter and dissipate his lead so that the apparent loser is able to come back strongly and eventually win.

An unwritten adage of golf is that "the green is always farther away than you think it is." This refers to the universal failure of golfers to take a strong enough club to get the ball up to the green or to the flagstick on the green. A corollary of this adage is that "the wind is always stronger than you think it is," referring to the similar inability of most golfers to judge the strength of the wind.

In putting, the rule is that "the break is always more than you figure it will be." In putting uphill "you are apt to come up short of the hole." In putting downhill "you are apt to go beyond the hole."

Although the putting cup usually will hold four or five golf balls comfortably, there is an odd superstition among golfers that once a player has holed his putt, he must remove it immediately or else "jinx" the next putter, who will not be able to get his ball in the hole. The reasoning, fallacious of course, is that the next ball putted into the cup will bounce out when it strikes the ball already at the bottom. It is only superstition, but you should be aware of it and prepared to remove your ball from the cup when you sink your putt. Another superstition you will encounter among golfers is that all balls lying near the cup be marked even if they are not truly in the line of another player's stroke toward the hole.

You will be playing with various golfers in your career, all of whom have differing attitudes and superstitions about golf. It is common politeness to observe them and understand them. You will become more of a "true golfer" if you do. My recommendation is that you yourself not become addicted to some of these odd golf superstitions. You will enjoy golf more if you get on with the game expeditiously and without wasting any time or motion.

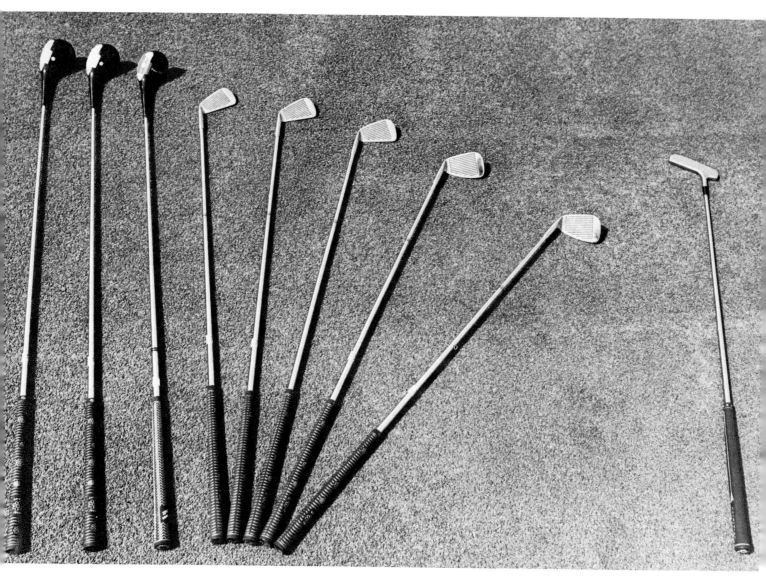

Pictured here is my recommendation for a completely adequate set of nine clubs for the beginner golfer: the 3-wood for driving, the 5-wood and 7-wood for lofted wood clubs, the 3-iron, 5-iron, 7-iron, 9-iron, sand wedge, and putter. After about a year of play with this set, the golfer may readily fill it in with the other numbered clubs, possibly including a driver, which should have the loft of a 2-wood or even a 3-wood. But learn to use this set competently before expanding your equipment.

chapter 28
THE EQUIPMENT

Let's talk about the equipment you will need for your golf game. Watching the televised golf tournaments might lead you to believe that you must have a veritable arsenal of tools, a monstrous bag, and all sorts of extras such as an umbrella for yourself and plastic covers for your bag when you encounter rain.

It is not true. You can enjoy beginning golf with a modest set of clubs and a small golf bag. If you happen to play in an area in which caddies are scarce and golf carts expensive, I recommend that you consider what the Scots call a "pencil bag," a light, simple canvas bag, well balanced and meant to be carried easily over your shoulder. Then you are ready to play at any time and any place. Just keep it in the trunk of your car along with your golf shoes. You

can stop at any nearby golf course and be on the first tee in a matter of minutes.

First, let's discuss the wood clubs you should have. The driver is an extremely straight-faced club with the least loft of all (11 degrees usually). It has the longest shaft, too. So it is not strange that for beginner golfers, and for many old-time players as well, the driver is the most difficult club to master. I say forget about the driver in your set, at least until you feel that you have achieved some proficiency with the other wood clubs and want to try for more distance off the tee.

My advice is to get a starter set of wood clubs, consisting of a 3-wood, a 5-wood, and a 7-wood. These clubs will have lofts of 16, 21, and 24 degrees, respectively, and will help you get the ball up in the air more

Here are two examples of extreme variations in the golfer's physical makeup. Ed Harris, who lost his left leg a few years ago in an automobile accident, has gone to 53-inch-long clubs and recently broke 80 at Atlantis Golf Club for the first time since his accident. Herb Miller, on the left, weighs only 90 pounds and swings a ladies' weight club very successfully. His low score is 87 for 18 holes.

easily. There is nothing more discouraging for the beginner than the shot that barely gets off the ground or fails completely to rise when struck. Later, as you progress with your game, you will be able to fit a driver into this wood set easily. All clubs these days have certain definite swing and weight characteristics, which your golf professional can analyze easily. Furthermore, if your beginner set is one made by a major manufacturer such as Spalding, Wilson, or McGregor, it is very likely that you will be able to fill in your set with a perfectly matched driver as well as matched irons as you need them.

For your irons, I recommend that for the first year, or possibly for two years, you use only the 5-iron, 7-iron, 9-iron, pitching wedge, sand wedge, and, of course, the putter. Those wood and iron clubs will give you an eight-club set that will weigh only nine pounds and, along with your light bag, will be very comfortable to handle.

I assure you from my personal experience of beginning golf in the 1920s with two wood clubs, a mid-iron, mashie, mashie-niblick, niblick (the ancient names for the 2-iron, 5-iron, 7-iron, and 9-iron), and putter, that I was able to play a most satisfactory game. Besides, thousands of other golfers used similar sets in those days and thrived on them. Furthermore, there are golfers all over the world playing with golf sets of no more than seven to nine clubs.

I would like to call your attention, too, to another benefit that will result from playing with the limited set of clubs I recommend. You soon will realize the importance of being able to hit some shots harder or softer than usual. You will gain greater control over your clubs if you are forced to hit a "soft" 7-iron in a situation that might prompt you to use an 8-iron if you had one.

Your bag should have a pair of pockets for your golf balls, tees, and golf glove.

Yes, I recommend that you use at least a left-hand golf glove when you play. Moreover, don't be embarrassed if you feel you need a right-hand glove as well. The beginner often has soft hands and skin that is easily blistered. Until you are accustomed to holding the golf club so that it does not slip in any way during the swing, you are apt to get some movement of the club in your hands at the top of the swing or, more likely, at the moment of impact when the torque of the clubhead hitting the ball tends to force open your grip. And that slippage in the fingers and hands will cause constant rubbing that may result in a blister. The golf glove you buy should be of good quality and skin-tight. You may pay a little more for it, but it will outwear and outlast a cheap glove. Be sure to buy a spare glove, too, for that rainy day when you will want a dry replacement.

Golf shoes with spiked cleats are a must. Rubber-soled golf shoes are very comfortable, I will agree, but the occasional rainstorm that you will encounter will make you glad that you chose the spikes. The spikes will hold on wet turf while the rubber soles will not. If you become a dedicated golfer, as I hope you will, you might find yourself playing golf two or three days in a row. If so, you should plan to have a second pair of spiked golf shoes ready in

the event that you get "rained out" while wearing your first pair of shoes. Golf shoes are difficult to dry after a thorough wetting, and there is no more unpleasant experience than donning still wet golf shoes from the day before. If you have a second pair, there is no problem.

When you buy your golf shoes, I recommend that you consider purchasing the best quality you can afford. A name brand such as Foot-Joy or Etonic is likely to remain more waterproof in the long run than one of the cut rate, no-name brands.

When you try on your golf shoes, be sure to bring along a pair of the short "half-socks" that many golfers find useful in helping to pad their feet inside the shoes. Another tip: don't buy pointed golf shoes because you like their looks. Buy a pair (or two) with moderately rounded toes. You will find them much more comfortable when you get into some awkward lies on sides of bunkers or hills. It is easier, too, to make a proper swing with the rounded-toe shoe. Your heel can rise from the ground and come down again without any variation.

What other equipment should you have? That larger side pocket on your bag can easily carry a light, zippered windbreaker. So get one for yourself, and make sure that it is large enough in the shoulders so that you can make a proper turn in your backswing without feeling constricted. There are many styles of jackets and windbreakers available. Pay a little more money and get a good one—you'll be glad you did when you are caught in a sudden, chilling rainstorm and your zipper works while your playing partner's does not!

You will need tees. My recommendation is that you buy extra-long tees for your use. For some strange reason, probably because they cost less, most golf tees are on the short side. There are tees made in lengths of 1⅛ to 2⅛ inches. You can always make a long tee shorter by pushing it into the ground a little farther, but you

Here is another picture that illustrates the wide variance in the physiques of golfers. The golfer on the left, Al Weller, is 5 feet, 6 inches tall, while Jack Van der Molen on the right is 6 feet, 4 inches tall. Al has a 32-inch-long arm, while Jack has a 40-inch arm. The golf clubs each one uses must be adapted to these physical characteristics.

cannot make a short tee longer when you encounter long grass and need some extra height.

For years now I have bought my golf tees in quantities of 1,000 from Dick Watson. I find that it is much less expensive to buy them that way than to buy a packet of 20 for 25 cents in the professional's shop. I like the extra-long 2⅛-inch tee in a bright yellow color, which is easy to find in the grass.

For the protection of your wood clubs, it is wise to have hood covers for them. These are little bags, or pouches, that fit over the heads and keep them from being scratched when you take an iron out of your bag, come up quickly, and strike the top of your 3-wood with the sharp edge of your iron. Individual hood covers are easily lost if you use them without some sort of a joining arrangement to tie them together. There are several types of connectors to solve this problem. I suggest that you buy connectors or else be reconciled to forever chasing your hood covers down previous fairways or in roughs where you have dropped them.

If you take pride in the condition of your golf clubs, they will last forever. Wipe them off with a soft rag after every round of golf, especially if moisture has gotten on them. If you do not use the services of a professional's golf shop, you should consider making your own golf club cleaning solution. It is easily done by mixing ¾ of a cup of trisodium phosphate with ¼ of a cup of powdered alum. A damp cloth or sponge dipped into this mixture will do an admirable cleaning job on grass-stained faces of irons and woods. Then rinse them off in water and dry them with a soft rag. If

you do not clean your clubs regularly, you will discover that the centers of the faces of your irons will begin to corrode. At that point, the only answer is a complete re-chroming, which is a nuisance and also expensive. However, re-chroming is often better than the original finish. The result may be a club that will outlast all the others in your set. The moral—take good care of your clubs!

Golf clubs are made in different weights and with varying swing characteristics called "swing-weights." These are based on mathematical formulas that are complicated. I suggest that you leave the decision of what weight club you should swing to the intelligence of your nearby member of the PGA, the Professional Golfers Association, who is trained to analyze your physical size and strength in order to fit you with suitable clubs.

By all means have confidence in your golf professional. He undoubtedly has seen hundreds of swings and has solved thousands of swing and equipment problems.

You will not go far wrong, however, if at first you use the standard or "regular" club with a swing-weight of D-1 or D-2. This is a fairly light club with some "help" in the shaft, or whippiness, which will get the clubhead through the ball at the last moment and probably give you the most satisfactory results. Strong golfers may use clubs with stiffer shafts and heavier heads. My recommendation is that you play your first year with the so-called "regular," or standard, clubs of a good manufacturer, and then, after you have learned to control them, consider making minor changes in their overall weight, swing-weight, and shaft flexibility.

Stormy weather gear! A good rain suit is a wise investment for the golfer who must occasionally play in the rain or the cold. The better suits do not "whistle" as the golfer makes his swing and are usually better ventilated than the cheaper variety. A waterproof hat is also a fine accessory. The umbrella, of course, is an absolute necessity, but be sure to get one with a wooden handle for safety's sake!

chapter 29
BAD-WEATHER GOLF

Bad-weather golf can be described as play in any weather that is abnormal, whether it is extremely cold, hot, wet, or windy. True, golfers always are anxious to start playing in a new spring season and hate to give it up in the fall. The result is that many times in your golfing career you will find yourself in the company of golf companions who prefer to play in bad weather rather than stop. You will play along with them, perhaps a bit unwillingly, but you will not want to be a spoilsport and the one to quit. Therefore, it is most useful to be prepared for all weather problems. If you are well-prepared and if you continue to play, and play with some success as well, there is a great deal of personal satisfaction that comes from conquering the elements. Let us examine a few of the many circumstances that can be classed as "bad-weather golf" and decide what preparations can be made in advance to deal with them.

The first thing to consider is the mental side of bad-weather golf. Remember that while you are going to be hampered by wind, rain, and cold, so, too, are your golfing companions. It follows that if you are better prepared for the elements than they, your game will prosper while theirs might not.

At some time in your golfing life, possibly many times, depending upon where you live and play, you will be caught in a sudden rainstorm. You should always be prepared not only for rain but also for the sudden drop in temperature that often follows the storm and causes you to be chilled and uncomfortable.

It is wise to carry a golf umbrella in your golf bag, one of those large colorful ones that give great protection from the elements. When you buy your first umbrella, get one with a plastic or wood shaft to lessen the possibility that you might turn into a human lightning rod.

Another item of equipment you should consider carrying with you at all times is a lightweight, nylon-zippered windbreaker. You can get one of these excellent products in a small carrying case that will not take up much room in your golf bag's side pocket. A sudden rain or sudden cold can be counteracted quickly when you have such a windbreaker. Be sure to get one that has lots of arm and shoulder room so that you will not be restricted in your swing even though you are wearing your jacket.

A complete rainsuit is expensive, but for the golfer who plays a great deal of golf, especially in club competitions where it is often necessary to continue play in the rain, such an outfit is an absolute necessity. These suits come in two pieces: the top is a waterproof jacket, and the other piece is a pair of rain pants that fit tightly around the ankles. If you buy a rain suit, be sure to buy one of good quality because the cheaper ones have an annoying habit of whistling or rubbing as you swing your arms. Get a suit that is as silent as possible because you do not want any unnecessary distraction as you swing.

Lightning is a serious danger to golfers on an exposed golf course. Beginner golfers usually are not as wary of lightning as old-timers are. If there is any threat of lightning near you, the U.S.G.A. strongly recommends that golfers suspend play and take refuge in the nearest safe place. Get away from your steel-shafted clubs because they may attract a lightning strike. Do not take refuge under a tall tree or on any high spot of terrain. If you are in serious danger and cannot find a safe place such as an equipment shed or nearby house, lie down flat on the ground until the danger is past. You may get wet, it is true, but you may save your life in the end.

It is useful to have an extra pair of waterproof golf shoes for your occasional bouts with rain or wet course conditions. You will find, however, that such shoes are very hot on your feet and can become quite uncomfortable. You will face the dilemma of either having wet feet from water getting into regular golf shoes or hot feet from watertight shoes. Here, too, is another reason for buying good golf shoes at the very beginning. Cheap golf shoes are the first to leak when they get wet, but even good golf shoes will lose their waterproof quality as they age. I personally believe the waterproof shoes are the better choice in wet weather but find that I am always glad to get out of them after their purpose has been served.

Carry an extra golf glove or two, as well, whenever there is a threat of wet weather. A soaked golf glove will not give you an effectively tight grip on the golf club. If you know you have an extra glove in your bag, you will have a relaxed feeling when you see no break in the rain clouds, your glove is getting wetter and wetter, and you must continue playing in a steady drizzle.

The best advice you can have about playing in the rain is "take it easy!" Your grip is apt to slip, your footing may become unsure, and your swing may have to be shortened as a result of donning a rain-jacket.

Accept the fact that you will not be able to hit the ball customary distances and adjust your strategy accordingly. The 4-par hole that might normally be a drive and a 5-iron shot might turn into a drive and a wood second shot or a long iron. In general, it is wise to assume that you will need "two numbers" more in the strength of your club to attain the same results you would get under favorable conditions. That means that when your brain registers the need for, say, a 7-iron to a green, your adjustment of two club numbers will result in your using a 5-iron instead. Furthermore, there should be no easing of the shot. You must swing your 5-iron and think "7-iron." There is a great tendency for most golfers who take stronger clubs than usually are required for a set distance to swing more easily, "give up" on the shot, and ruin the hole completely.

It is very important when you are playing in the rain to make sure that you hit the ball as flush on the center of the club blade as possible. That is why it is good to shorten your swing and swing "within yourself," meaning, don't overswing; don't try to overpower the ball or hit it harder than usual just because you are getting less distance on your shots. Let the additional power come from using a stronger club rather than a stronger swing.

It is obvious that when you are playing in the rain, it will be best to avoid the rough if you can. If you do get into the rough, it is often better to use your lofted wood club rather than an iron to extricate yourself. There is something about the design of a wood club that enables the head to get through long, wet grass better than an iron can.

Try to swing with rhythm in the rain and you will be surprised at your success. It is a great thrill for any golfer to beat the elements. You can do it if you approach the situation in an intelligent fashion and work with the rain rather than allow it to beat you.

Here I am demonstrating a wrist curl, using the steering wheel of my golf cart. This is a great exercise for strengthening the wrists. If you do this exercise faithfully every day, you will put many yards on your drives. You can use the steering wheel of your car. Remember to hold extreme tension for seven successive seconds. Once a day is all you need, according to experts on isometric exercises!

chapter 30

EXERCISES FOR GOLF

While it is true, in general, that exercises that strengthen the entire body are useful for golfers, in my opinion special attention should be paid by the beginner golfer to exercises designed to strengthen muscles used in the golf swing. I refer to the strength required in the left hand, left wrist, and left forearm to withstand the force of the impact with the golf ball.

ISOMETRIC EXERCISES

In our discussion of the proper grip, we pointed out the necessity for the last three fingers of the left hand to remain in control of the club so that it does not turn away at the torque, or turning movement, applied to the clubhead by the weight of the golf ball as it strikes the clubface.

Finger, Hand, and Wrist Strength

The first and most important exercises for the beginner golfer are aimed at increasing the finger and hand strength of his left hand. For this purpose you should use a simple rubber ball small enough to fit the palm of the hand easily. There are other rubber grips meant for the same purpose, which can be bought in nearly any store that sells sports goods.

The method of practice is to hold the rubber ball loosely in your left hand and then suddenly close your hand on it, giving particular emphasis to the clenching of the last three fingers. Hold your hand closed tightly while you count from "one thousand and one" up to "one thousand and seven." This is an isometric exercise technique that is very effective. You should carry out this finger practice daily. Keep a rubber ball on the seat of your car, one in your desk at work, and one in plain view at home so that by seeing it you will be encouraged to use it.

This "pulling out" exercise is great for strengthening the upper arms and forearms. It can be turned into a wrist curl from the side for a wrist-strengthening exercise. I recommend that you make it a habit to do these exercises every time your automobile must wait for a traffic signal. Count to seven seconds for full isometric benefit.

There are many twisting devices used to strengthen wrists and forearms. A simple one that you can make for yourself at little cost consists of a round bar of wood, some sash-cord or line, and a weight. Take an old broom handle and cut it to about an eighteen-inch length. Drill it at the center so that you can insert one end of a line about four feet long, or long enough to extend from your shoulder to the floor. At the working end of the line suspend either an iron weight such as weight lifters use, which can be bought at a sports store, or improvise by using a plastic bottle filled with water.

At first use five to seven pounds of weight, and then increase it to ten to fifteen pounds. The exercise is to wind the cord up, turn by turn, from the floor until it is chest high, and then to let it down, turn by turn, until it is once more on the floor. This exercise, a simple one, will strengthen your wrists and forearms remarkably.

For increasing the strength of your left arm and left side, I recommend that you get a mock golf club with weight increased to 26 ounces at the end. There are such practice clubs for sale in golf merchandising stores, but you can easily make your own by drilling the head of an old wood club and filling it with lead to the proper weight. For a shorter club, you can use an old, broken shaft complete with its original grip and add the weight to the shaft end. I, personally, have used this style of practice club indoors in the winter and vouch for its effectiveness in building the necessary golf muscles in hand, arm, and, for that matter, the entire body. Exercises to be done with the short, heavy club are as follows.

1. Practice one-arm, left-hand "takeaways." In this move you concentrate on a firm left hand and the movement of the body "all-in-one-piece" to a position where the club is at shoulder height. Just "take the club away" in this exercise, time after time after time, to exactly the same stopping point in the backswing. The purpose, of course, is to standardize every swing and help you develop rhythm.

2. Next, practice the takeaway plus the downswing. At the point of imaginary impact in the downswing, you should attempt to stop the club in mid-air. You will find this very difficult to do. The weight of the club is in motion, and it wants to stay in motion. All the muscles of the hand, wrist, and left arm will resist the stopping action, and with that resistance you will be building great strength.

3. Most certainly, practice your entire swing with the weighted club. When you are using a practice club, you will find it useful to swing before a mirror. By positioning yourself at the far right-hand side of the mirror, you can visually check whether or not you are swaying to the right or left as you swing. Obviously, if your mirrored reflection moves to the right or left, it is an indication that you are not obeying the "steady head" rule and must work on that flaw in your game.

SPECIAL EXERCISES FOR A BETTER SWING

I cannot overemphasize the importance of the special exercises that will help you build the sound, strong physical foundation of a good golf swing. You may practice these body movements and strengthening routines in the privacy of home, in your basement recreation room, in your bedroom before a mirror, or in a swimming pool or lake.

It will be wise for you to buy one or more of the practice devices you will find for sale in the advertisements of such popular magazines as *Golf Digest* and *Golf.* One of your best buys is the practice club known as "The Grip." It has a short-

Here is an exercise that Horton Smith recommended in order for the golfer to get the feeling of compactness and rhythm in his swing. He felt that it emphasized the important role of the lower body and allowed the golfer to concentrate on a proper body and shoulder turn in the shot.

Here is the finish of the club-behind-the-back exercise. This move should be made with the same rapidity that you use in your normal full swing. Do it with rhythm and increasing acceleration. Imagine that you are striking the ball with a real clubhead. Be sure to keep the steady head position throughout the exercise.

ened shaft that can be swung inside the house without striking the ceiling or furniture, but you must be careful with your aim, of course. "The Grip" is made of a molded material with exactly the proper indentations for your fingers in a golf grip that is neither too "strong" nor too "weak," that is, a grip that might eventually be suitable for you.

If you will handle "The Grip" every day and swing it faithfully, you will accustom yourself to the feel of a proper golf grip, and when you swing your own club, you will find that your hands automatically assume familiar and correct positions. It is really too bad that the U.S.G.A. forbids the use of a practice device such as this in regular play because it is "contrary to the spirit of golf." Perhaps someday the rule will change; until then I recommend that you use the device regularly in your practice routines.

You may practice your body movements in a swimming pool, too, with excellent results. The water provides strong resistance to your hands, arms, and body in much the same way that the heavy prac-

tice clubs do. I recommend that you stand in the shallower part of the swimming pool so that the water is about chest high. Perform the "push-back" and "pull-down" exercises at least ten times in succession. You also might wish to practice the quick return of your left side to the ball. Other arm-strengthening exercises should be carried out, too.

In your bedroom or recreation room, work especially hard on perfecting a golf swing that evidences steady head movement. If you have a full-length mirror, orient yourself so that your eyes are reflected in the mirror from the far right-hand edge of the mirror frame. Then, as you practice your swing, you can monitor your head position out of the corner of your eyes. If you move at all away from the steady head position, the fault will be evident immediately because your reflection in the glass will disappear.

In outdoor practice you may use the same idea by swinging "down sun," that is, with the sun behind you. Any faulty movement of your head will be clearly noticeable in your shadow.

This is the 5-iron shot in heavy rough with the ball "sitting up" pretty well. The iron club is the safest to use, but it also is possible that you might be able to use a lofted wood club as well. One of the problems in using the wood, however, is the tendency of the golfer to dig too far under the ball and thus "sky" the ball off the top of the club. Unless it is absolutely necessary because of the strategic situation, it usually is wisest to play it safe and get out with the iron. You will be surprised how far you can advance the ball with a swing that is really not trying for distance.

chapter 31

WHEN YOU ARE IN TROUBLE

Every golfer gets into trouble at some time during a round of golf, even the most proficient professional player. Most certainly, golf would not be the attractive game that it is if it did not offer its unique hazards to the golfer: the trees, the longer grass in the rough at the edges of the fairway, the water in ponds and creeks, the sand and grass bunkers, the undulations of terrain that force the player to take an uneven and often an unbalanced stance.

But part of the triumph of golf lies in successfully conquering those hazards. Let us consider a few "trouble situations" and discuss the best ways to deal with them. The adage that applies to trouble shots is: "When you are in trouble, the first thing to do is to get out of trouble." Sometimes you find yourself so deep in the woods or heavy rough that the only thing you can consider is getting your ball back onto the fairway, or at least near the fairway, where you then

can advance it toward the green with some hope of success.

So the first thing to do when you are in deep trouble is to find the broadest opening through the trees to the fairway and take that route out with whatever club will get you there. Or, finding yourself in deep rough, take your heaviest wedge, swing through the long grass, and get the ball out onto the fairway if you can. The corollary of this adage is: "Don't be hungry and don't take the long chance in getting out of trouble." You may find yourself in even deeper trouble if your ball ricochets off a tree. In other words, it is wiser to take the easiest route out of trouble and sacrifice any thought of gaining distance.

In deep rough you will find that an iron will get through the grass better than a wood club. However, in light rough, oddly enough, the reverse situation is true. Your 5-wood or 7-wood will work there better

This picture shows clearly why it so often is easier to use a 5-wood (or even a 7-wood) on a ball "down in the rough." The wood clubhead seems to get through to the ball better than an iron club would, and the loft gets it up quickly and safely.

than the long iron club. (See photos.) When you are faced with a shot out of deep rough, it seems almost inevitable that you will overexert yourself and try to hit too hard with your right hand, thinking that it will require a mighty blow to extricate the ball. You must resist this tendency to over-swing and over-hit with your right hand because it will pull the shot to your left, or you might even mis-hit it completely.

Pay careful attention to your balance while making trouble shots. In order to lessen the slowing effect of long grass behind the ball, the swing should be executed with a more upright takeaway of the club. You do not want to hit any more of that obstructing grass on the way back down to the ball than is absolutely necessary. Your weight should remain more left-sided than usual. Your follow through must be vigorous, even exaggerated. "Staying down to the ball" is most necessary for success on this shot.

Many times you will find yourself in the deep grass beyond a green, usually down a slope or hillside. Here, your strategy will be to use your sand wedge or pitching wedge, depending upon the length of the shot. Whatever you do, get your ball up and out of the trouble. Temporarily disregard the flagstick position; that is, do not try to play the shot too carefully, "too cozy," as the expression goes. Because if you do, you will inevitably underestimate the resisting force of the long grass and not hit the shot hard enough. The result will leave you still in deep grass faced with practically the same tactical situation that you had before you "fluffed" the shot. So hit the ball harder than you think you should when coming out of heavy rough beyond a green. You will be surprised when that strategy results in exactly the right power applied to both grass and ball, a successful extrication from trouble, and a possible "save" of a par or bogey.

Sometimes it is necessary to violate a basic rule of the good swing in order to get the result you want. Here I am illustrating the necessity of "picking the club up fast" in my backswing in order to strike a more descending blow at impact and thus keep the trajectory lower than normal. The hands are held ahead of the ball, and usually the swing is curtailed a bit in the backswing.

chapter 32
SPECIAL SITUATIONS

HITTING THE BALL HIGHER OR LOWER

The trajectory of your golf shot can be raised or lowered with any club if you understand the principles involved. We have shown you the "magic movement" of the golf ball off the face of the golf club. (See photo.) In that case we used a 5-iron with a loft of 32 degrees. The movement of the ball off the 5-iron face at that precise angle necessarily depends upon the clubface striking the ball at what would be considered a "normal angle," the angle that is apparent when the club is fully and squarely soled on a line off the inside of the golfer's left foot at the bottom of the swing. This also presumes that the golfer's hands are held at an angle that is straight down the shaft of the club, neither "in front of" nor "in back of" that straight line from the golfer's left shoulder, left arm, and left hand down to the clubhead. Altering the relative position of the ball at rest from its so-called normal position off the inside

of the left foot will result in a different approach angle of the clubhead as it strikes the ball.

Here are the basic rules: move the ball forward to raise your trajectory; move it backward to lower it. The hands are allowed to help sometimes in these situations, so here are the rules about hand positions: move your hands back, behind the ball, to raise the trajectory; move them forward, in front of the ball, to lower it. (See the photos.)

Turning the clubface of any club clockwise is called "opening the face." This gives the club more loft and, for example, will turn a 5-iron into a 5½-iron or even a 6-iron. Turning the clubface counterclockwise "closes the face," reduces its loft, and turns a 5-iron into a 4½- or 4-iron.

There are other modifications, too, that you can make in order to help change the loft of your club in order to hit a higher or lower shot than normal. For the high shot,

To hit the ball high, position it forward in your swing. Note that the hands are behind the line running from the toe to the ball position. With hands behind the ball, you increase the loft of your club, and the shot will travel in a higher trajectory than it would if the hands were brought more forward on the line toward the ball. This position would be used if the golfer wanted to hit his driver (or other wood club) higher than normal.

widen your stance a few inches. That means move your right foot a few inches to the right. This can be a dangerous move because it changes the basic swing pattern you have developed. It may cause you to lose your ability to turn your hips away from the ball. If widening your stance does not work for you, forget about it and use the other two moves—ball forward in your stance and hands back.

For the lowered trajectory, move the ball back from its normal position and at the same time move your hands forward.

Experiment with these two situations. Notice how the clubface gains and loses loft as you move your hands forward and backward from your usual position and how your hand position also affects the loft by opening and closing the face of the club.

You will find, too, that there is a limit on the distance forward or backward that you can move the ball without really missing the shot badly. The farther you play the ball forward in your stance, the more difficult it will be to "stay with the ball," that is, get your clubface squarely on it. The reverse is true when moving the ball back in your stance. In order to hit the ball on the line you want, you will find it necessary to close the clubface. Then, you will reach a point where the closing is so severe that you won't have much chance of getting the ball off the ground.

Remember, when you increase or decrease the loft of your club, you will be changing the distance potential of that club. Adjust your thinking in this way: "In opening the face of my 5-iron to hit the ball higher, it will turn into a 6-iron. I regularly hit my 6-iron 140 yards; therefore, I had better plan on 140 yards, not the 150 yards I usually get with my 5-iron." In that way you will never be hooked into thinking that you will get your normal distance with a club altered by increasing its loft.

These high and low shots border on "trick shots" in golf. It may be several years before you are able to do them, but you should know about them. For your first year or two, concentrate on "normal" shots rather than confuse yourself with variations in your swing that may upset your whole game.

PLAYING UNEVEN LIES

When playing the ball off hilly lies, there are some simple adjustments to make in your stance, grip, and swing. They are vital, too, for the absence of any one of them

Here is a downhill lie with the left foot lower than the right. The key here is to concentrate on keeping your balance as you swing and "go down after the ball," along the line of the terrain, as you hit it. There must be no pulling up whatsoever. Sometimes, too, you are better off to shorten your swing under a severe situation such as this.

will cause the shot to fail.

First, the golfer must be most careful to retain his balance during the swing, even to the point where it may become necessary to shorten the swing drastically rather than take the chance of being thrown off balance while one foot is higher or lower than the other.

On a downhill lie it is obvious that if the club is taken away in normal fashion, it will be scraped along the ground. Therefore, the golfer must use a more upright

swing. The clubface should be hooded, that is, closed slightly in a counterclockwise fashion. The golfer also must attempt to follow the ball down the hill with his stroke. This will, of course, be difficult to do, but if it is not done, there is a strong tendency to hit the ground before hitting the ball or to top the ball and "foozle" the shot completely. Since your club will have less effective loft as a result of keeping the face closed as it "goes after the ball," it is useful to use a club from one to two numbers higher on downhill lies. Select a 7-iron

Sometimes the downhill lie is so severe that a wood club cannot be used. It will not loft the ball high enough to raise it in its flight. Then the choice has to be a more lofted iron and the sacrifice of distance in order to advance the ball successfully. Remember the adage, "When you are in trouble, the first thing to do is get out of trouble!" Don't be greedy and try to get distance when there is a chance of missing the shot completely.

Here is an action shot of a successful stroke at a ball from a severely downhill lie. Notice my obvious effort to "stay with the shot" by letting the clubhead follow the contour of the terrain. It is clear, too, that I have kept my head steady until long after the ball is on its way.

when the shot seems to call for a 5-iron. Shots that come out of downhill lies are apt to fade, that is, move from left to right in their flight. You must allow for this in your calculations of direction by aiming to the left of your target.

On an uphill lie you should play the ball off your left heel. Try not to pick up the club quickly as you take it away. Swing with the terrain, that is, follow through straight up the hill after the ball. Since this shot effectively increases the loft of your club, take a club that is stronger (lower) by a number or two in order to get the distance you normally would expect.

Let's consider a 5-iron shot from an uphill lie. By a 5-iron shot we mean the distance a 5-iron usually travels. Let's say that distance is 150 yards. But because the lie is uphill, the club loft will be increased, and the ball will fly higher and fall short of its regular distance. The solution is to use a 4-iron or even a 3-iron. The distance you get will depend upon the way you hit the shot and whether your hands are even with the ball at impact or lagging behind it, a situation that would increase the club loft even more.

On sidehill lies where the golfer's feet are below the ball, your swing will be "flattened," somewhat like the arc of a baseball swing. You must shorten your grip on the club. And, most important to realize, the club loft will tend to send the golf ball to the golfer's left. A deep-faced iron will do this more readily than a shallow-faced iron. Plan on the ball going to the left of wherever you think it will, and you often will be correct. Most beginner golfers underestimate this correction. If anything, overestimate the correction you will need because, in addition, the golfer often seems to lose his balance to the left and will pull the ball even farther in that direction.

On sidehill lies where the golfer's feet are above the ball, you must stand closer to the ball. Hood, or close, the clubface slightly. Take one club longer than the shot ordinarily calls for. And stand by for a fade, or push, to the right of your intended line.

There are many varieties of hillside lies, requiring different positions for the feet. Only years of experience will give you confidence in playing them. If you can find a practice area where you can simulate some of these situations, it will be of great help. For if you are able to hit the golf ball out of difficult lies, it stands to reason that you will be able to hit it well off the tee and out of good lies.

Here is an illustration of a sidehill lie in which the ball is well below the feet of the golfer. As in all trouble shots, balance is very important. There is a tendency for the golfer to fall forward as he makes this shot, so the weight should be kept well back on the heels. This shot will be "pushed," too, to the right. Therefore, plan to aim to the left of your target to allow the normal push of the shot to bring it on line.

On this sidehill lie the ball is well above the golfer's feet. Remember that you will have a tendency to "pull" this shot to the left, so allow for the pull by aiming to the right of the target. Just as it is important in every shot, here it is vital that the golfer "stay with the shot," that is, not raise his body as he goes through the ball. Balance, too, is very important, so swing easily in a situation such as this in order to keep your equilibrium.

WIND

Here is Glenn Johnson demonstrating a tee-shot with the wind. Note that he has teed his ball up higher than he would normally and that he has moved the position of his ball more toward his left toe. This will ensure a sweeping hit that will drive the ball higher in the air where the wind can "help" it more.

chapter 33

PLAYING IN THE WIND

There are, basically, two kinds of winds, those that help the golfer and those that hinder him. The first kind, the helping winds, are those that come from the rear quadrants to the right and left as well as from directly behind. Picture a clock dial and envision any wind coming from the direction between 4:00 and 8:00 and you'll get the idea.

Now picture winds on that same clock dial coming from between 10:00 and 2:00 and you will understand the hurting winds, ones that will take distance off your ball. The winds that come from 2:00 through 4:00 and from 8:00 through 10:00 do not so much hinder the flight of the ball as affect its movement to one side or the other.

Let's talk about the helping winds first. They are often a pleasure to encounter because they really do help you hit some incredibly long shots. I remember playing the "Long Hole In," the 527-yard four-

teenth at St. Andrews soon after the Open championship of 1970. A ranger told me he estimated the wind that day at more than 40 miles per hour. I wanted to play the "Tiger Tee" the professionals had used for the event. It was built out on a promontory above the watery Firth of Forth. The wind was coming from directly behind me. I teed my ball up a little higher than usual and fortunately hit it flush on the center of my clubface. That drive measured over 300 yards when my caddie and I checked it later. The second shot to the green took only an iron, and I scored a triumphant birdie 4.

The first rule for playing tee shots with the wind behind you is to tee the ball up higher than you usually do. Secondly, play it a half-inch farther off your left toe in your address. That will ensure a swing that catches the ball more on the upswing, increases the effective loft of your drive, and

WIND

Glenn Johnson, five times Michigan Amateur Champion, is demonstrating a drive into a headwind. The ball should be teed somewhat lower in this situation, the swing should be a bit slower, and every possible effort made to meet the ball precisely in the center of the clubface. The ball is sometimes played back in the stance, that is, a little to the right of its normal position in order to increase the "knocked down" effect of the club. As a beginner, I advise you to try to play the shot in normal position, and as your game progresses try variations in positioning the ball.

puts the ball higher in the air than usual where the wind can do its work of helping. On other than tee-shots you should plan to use a club with one or two numbers more loft.

The rule for playing tee-shots against the wind is just the opposite. Tee the ball slightly lower. You may play it in the normal position off your left toe or, if you can make a good swing, a little back toward the center of your stance. But be certain that you "go through the shot" with your hands and wrists. If you allow a left wrist

break on a shot into the wind, you will be in trouble because the ball will go up into the air and be much more affected by the influence of the wind. Into the wind, too, you should concentrate on a clean, flush hit on the face of the club. The wind seems to know when the ball has not been hit "purely" and grabs it and kills it or else emphasizes the hook or slice spin and sends it farther off-line than it would have gone if there had been no wind. Against the wind, on shots other than tee-shots, you should plan to play a club with one to two numbers less loft in order to keep the ball "down" where it will be less affected by the wind.

On shots with the wind coming from the side, let's say from 2:00 to 4:00 and from 8:00 to 10:00 on the clock dial, my advice is to "join" the wind. That means that you should let it help you. Here's an example. You normally slice your iron shots a few yards from the 150-yard distance. You have a 15-mile wind coming from the 10:00 position. You will have to figure that a 10-yard slice will probably turn into a 25-yard slice because of "help" from the wind. Therefore, aim 25 yards to the left instead of making your regular correction of 10 yards. Remember the corrections for wind against you and wind behind you, as well. If the left-hand wind were from 10:00, you might use a 4-iron instead of a 5-iron. If it were from 8:00, you might use the 6-iron.

I hope this explanation helps you to understand the basic rules for playing in the wind. If you find it hard to judge such shots, and you will, I would like to assure you that all golfers find wind shots difficult to play. Several years ago the PGA championship was played at the nearby PGA course in Florida. The wind one day was about 25 miles per hour directly against the players on the incoming nine. I watched at least 20 of the top professionals play their second shots to a short par 4 hole. Only *one* player was able to judge the wind that day and get his ball up to the hole. Who was it? Sam Snead, the veteran campaigner!

Shots on windy days are difficult, but if you successfully outwit the wind, make it help you to a good score, you will find that there is no more rewarding pleasure in golf!

Glenn Johnson demonstrates a shot into a crosswind from left to right. His stance is normal and the positioning of the ball is normal, off the inside of his left shoe. He will try to hit the ball "flush" so that any spin on the ball will not be accentuated. He will correct his aim to "square away" on a line to the left of his target, thus allowing the wind to "help" his ball.

Wandering right elbow. The right elbow sometimes begins to get away from the right side of the golfer's body if he exaggerates the action of taking the club straight back from the ball in his takeaway. If you concentrate on a feeling of compactness between your right arm and right side and keep your elbow pointing toward the ground, you will eliminate this fault or at least keep it under good control.

Swaying forward in the golf swing is a horrible fault, and it usually produces disastrous results. Here I am pictured demonstrating how a sway to the left appears in relation to the original ball position. It is evident that the steady head position has been lost and that the golfer has moved, or swayed, to his left. The usual result of this fault is a ball that goes badly off-line to the right, as the clubhead never becomes square to the target line.

chapter 34
A PHOTO ALBUM OF SWING FAULTS

Swaying to the right. It is clear in this shot that the steady head position has been lost. It is possible for the golfer to regain it by a sway back to the ball, but the necessary windup of the body cannot be accomplished properly from this position, and considerable power will be lost in the swing. I recommend that you practice swinging "down sun" in order to detect any movement of your head as you swing. The steady head is a most important part of the effective golf swing.

Letting go at the top of the backswing. Here is an exaggerated view of this bad fault. Jokingly, it sometimes is called "playing the piccolo" for obvious reasons. The golfer relaxes the last three fingers of his left hand and allows the momentum of the clubhead to force them open. In order to complete the swing, it is necessary to re-grip the club, an action called "snatching" at the club. The result is a jerky, erratic swing because sometimes the fingers do not re-grip where they were originally. The only way to eliminate this fault is to work on hand and finger strengthening exercises and not rush the swing, which creates overpowering momentum in the club.

The broken left arm is a common fault among golfers. This fault inserts an extra move, a variable, into the backswing, namely, the necessity of re-straightening the arm before returning the clubhead to its original starting place. Some golfers can recover properly, but my advice is never to allow the habit to develop. Work diligently on keeping your left elbow straight and firm but not rigid or extremely tensed. The result will be a compact, effective golf swing that returns the club to the ball every time in the same way and to the same place for proper impact.

Picking up the club too quickly. An examination of this photo reveals that although the club is only a few inches into the takeaway, it is already several inches above the ground. This is a common fault and a most serious one. The clubhead should sweep back almost parallel to the ground in order to permit the full windup of the body in the swing.

(Above), hands held too low at the address position forces the golfer to stoop over the ball too much. The clubhead, too, is forced into an unnatural "flat" impact position, which may cause the heel of the club to strike the ground first with erratic results. Some good golfers, notably Hubert Green, have very low hand positions at the start of their swings, but they compensate for the error by corrections as their swings progress.

(Above), standing too erect at the ball in address position. This stiff posture is conducive to an arm and upper body swing with little or no involvement of the lower body, a so-called "disjointed" swing that never achieves a unified arms, legs, and body "one-piece" action. The correction is to "sit down" more to the ball by bending the knees and lowering the hands somewhat.

(Below), dragging the clubhead back with the hands rather than letting them act as a unit with the body is another often seen swing fault. It might be called a faulty wrist break at address, too. Notice that although the hands have moved the clubhead, my body has not budged. This is definitely not an "all-in-one-piece" swing. It is what I call a disjointed swing. The hands and the body should begin the backswing at the same time.

chapter 35
SAFETY ON THE COURSE

There are many dangerous places and things on a golf course. You should be aware of them and never put yourself into any situation that might result in personal injury to yourself or anyone else.

First and foremost in importance is the golf club itself. You must always be wary of the practice swings of other golfers. Some golfers are completely unaware of the dangerous arcs of their swings. On a first tee, where golfers are apt to warm up indiscriminately, there is particular danger that you might be struck by another person's club. It follows, too, that you should be careful where and how you take your practice swings.

Another danger area on a golf course is that arc from about 85 degrees to directly forward on the right side of any right-handed golfer or from 275 degrees to directly forward on the left side of a left-handed golfer. This area is known as the "shank zone," the arc within which a ball that is mis-hit may come darting off the shank, or hosel, of the golf club. If you will examine an iron club carefully, you will understand why a ball that is struck on the hosel will be forced to the right at an oblique angle. For your own safety, never allow yourself to be in "shank area" when another golfer is making his stroke. And never allow another person to enter your

danger area as you play your stroke.

A golf ball is extremely hard and achieves a speed of more than one hundred miles per hour in flight. It will ricochet at the same speed if it strikes a hard object such as a rock or a tree trunk. I can assure you that if a golf shot does ricochet, it will happen so fast that your defensive reactions will not have time to function. If you are in the way, you will be hit and may suffer serious injury to an eye, your face, or your body. It is not unknown for a golfer to be struck in the eye and blinded by such a ricocheting shot.

So be very careful when you are confronted with a golf shot that requires you to aim near trees or any other object that might act as a backboard reflector. Be careful when you are near another golfer who is attempting such a shot because his errant ball might come back and strike you. The best thing to do, I have found, is simply to remove yourself far enough from the danger so that you are completely safe or else stay far enough away so that you have that second or so to dodge the shot. Another trick I have used successfully (I never have been hit by such a shot, incidentally) is the maneuver I call "cowering," or hiding behind the nearest large tree trunk or golf cart until the danger is past.

chapter **36**

HOW TO PLAY ON ALMOST ANY COURSE

You can play golf on any one of thousands of golf courses all over the world if you understand how to gain entrée to them. Golf courses fit into three categories of membership. The first, called the private club, is comprised of a group of members that have banded together to own and operate their own club on a private basis. Play is restricted to the members, their families, and their invited guests. The second type of club is called "semi-private" or "semi-public" (both terms here have the same meaning). They offer a seasonal or continuing membership to golfers and their families but also welcome the public or non-invited guest golfers on a daily play basis. The third style of golf club operation is the truly public golf course operated by a municipality that invites all golfers to play, usually for a modest "green fee," the name for payment for a round of golf.

You will have little or no difficulty arranging to play on the public or semi-public golf courses. When you are traveling, carry your golf clubs with you and be ready for any opportunity to play golf that presents itself along the way. You can make inquiries of the local inhabitants about the nearest and best golf club and, with a phone call ahead of time to the Pro Shop, usually can make arrangements for a designated starting time, an electric cart or caddie, or a pull-cart if you wish to use one. The professional in charge of the Pro Shop is always pleased to arrange for playing partners for visiting golfers. It is common courtesy, of course, to buy your golf balls, tees, or a new golf cap from such a Pro Shop.

Although the term "private" referring to a golf club means that you, as a non-member, are not truly "invited" to play golf at such a course, there are many ways in which to circumvent this restriction. It

undoubtedly is true that the finest golf lay-outs in the world are under the control of private groups. Still, it often is possible to obtain the necessary introduction to a private golf club and thus be invited to play the course. The first step is to have an established handicap at your "home course," whether it be a public or private one. That is your passport to golf legitimacy. It is a little wallet-sized card issued by your local golf association, attesting to the fact that you do, indeed, possess a certain handicap. I, personally, believe that the lower handicap player has an advantage in this regard because the private club will give a heartier welcome to a golfer who will not cut up their course than to the higher handicap player who might carve out large divots and take more strokes and more time in playing his round.

The second step in securing an invita-tion to a private club is to be known to a member of the club who will "sponsor" your request to play. Some of the most restricted private golf courses require that a member of the club accompany you on your golf round. Some do not. A letter of introduction from the secretary of your local golf association to the head professional of the private club often will be sufficient to receive the required invitation.

Golf in Scotland, England, and Ireland, too, is governed by much the same rules of "invitation to play." There are golf reference books in your local library that give the names, addresses, green fees, and conditions of play for golf courses all over the world. A letter of introduction sent in advance to the club secretary of nearly any of the world's great golf courses will bring you a favorable answer and an invitation to play.

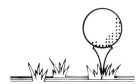

chapter 37

KEEPING A SCORECARD

Part of becoming a well-rounded golfer includes learning how to keep a good scorecard. To the other members of a foursome, having an efficient, accurate scorekeeper is one of the extra pleasures of golf. With a little practice and the knowledge of a few scorekeeping tricks, you can become an excellent scorekeeper.

When you begin to play golf, you undoubtedly will find that your scores are, as they say, "in the 100s," meaning scores of 100 strokes or more for 18 holes. Do not be dismayed if at first your score is as high as 120 or more. However, your improvement will be rapid, and soon you will find yourself in the low 100s range. Golfers who score in the low 100s often keep their scores by counting themselves as so many strokes over or under 6s. That is a method of computing your standing during a round so that you can figure your chances of scoring "even 6s," or 9 x 6 = 54 strokes for 9 holes, or 108 for 18 holes.

Let's look at an example of this type of scoring because the theory applies equally well to "even 5s," "even 4s," and par. If you should score 9 straight 6s, obviously you would have 54 strokes for the 9 holes. So if you are, say, 3 under 6s through the sixth hole, it would mean that if you finished your 9 holes with 3 more 6s, you would have 54 - 3, or 51, for the 9 holes. Your card, through the sixth hole, would look like this: 5, 7, 4, 6, 5, 6. You would read your card, hole by hole, as "one under 6s, even 6s, two under 6s, still two under 6s, three under 6s, still three under 6s," and so on.

Sooner or later you will begin to challenge the 100 mark and use 5s as your scoring target. 5 x 9 = 45 and two 45s = 90, a score that is, of course, 10 under the 100 mark. Therefore, in order to "break 100," meaning score less than 100 strokes, all you need to do is achieve a score of "9 over 5s." That means you can score a 49 and a

50 for a 99 total score, with the 49 being "4 over 5s" and the 50 being "5 over 5s," or a total of "9 over 5s."

Eventually your scores might improve so much that you will count them in relation to 4s in the same way or in relation to par.

The scorecard reads:

Par: 4 4 3 5 4 3 5 4 4   36
Score: 5 5 3 6 4 3 4 4 4   38

This is read, hole by hole, as "1 over par, 2 over par, 2 over par, 3 over par, 3 over par, 3 over par, 2 over par, 2 over par, and 2 over par" for a total of 2 strokes over the par of 36 for a score of 38.

When you are keeping a scorecard for a foursome, it is the mark of a good scorekeeper to keep a running total of the medal scores of all the players so that as you come to the last hole you are able to say, for example: "You and I, Joe, are even on

our medal scores at 2 over 5s, and, Bill, you and Tom need 4s for 49s."

Some golfers keep the running medal score by using dots placed alongside the hole-by-hole totals. Two tiny dots, for example, alongside the score for the seventh hole on this scorecard denote a score of 2 over 5s at that point:

Score: 7·· 5·· 4· 6·· 4 ·6··

It is possible that you may not need to use these scoring tricks. You may be an excellent mathematician, able to glance at a running score and add it up in your mind quickly. The important point is to keep an accurate scorecard for yourself and for your playing partners. Devise your own scoring "tricks" or use some of these suggested shortcuts, but resolve to become the best scorekeeper in your club. The accomplishment will add immeasurably to your pleasure of golf.

chapter **38**

READING ABOUT GOLF

As a beginner golfer, one of the best things you can do besides seeking out professional instruction is to begin an educational study program in the literature of golf. For more than one hundred years the best golfers of the world have been writing their observations and analyses of the golf swing. In my own library, for example, I have a marvelous old golf book published in 1899 and written by Horace G. Hutchinson, who was the British Amateur Champion of 1886 and 1887. All the great golfers of his day are pictured and their swing methods described. Among them are the first "Big Three" of golf, Harry Vardon, James Braid, and J.H. Taylor. Surprisingly enough, there are solid tips from these wonderful players, tips that are as applicable today as they were in the 1890s.

I suggest that you visit your nearest library and read all the golf books you find on the shelves. Your enthusiasm for golf will be increased, and you will become even more a "true golfer" when you know the history of the game and have an understanding of the golf swing as it has been described by the best players. Plan to read and even buy, if your budget allows you to do so, several of the classic books on golf so that you will have them for reference and rereading. You will find that your understanding of the swing will increase as

you play the game more, so a concept that seems beyond your comprehension today will become clear a year later as you continue to develop your game and your knowledge of it.

I recommend that you read the several golf books written by Robert T. Jones, Jr., the famous "Bobby" Jones. He was a gentleman golfer and a golf scholar as well. You will enjoy his books immensely. For a classic instructional book, you should read Ben Hogan's *Five Secrets of Golf.* The techniques it teaches may be beyond the beginner's ability, but for a clear explanation of what the golf swing should do, it is an excellent text.

There are several golf magazines you should read regularly. *Golf Digest* and *Golf,* which are monthly magazines, are both well written and most informative. They often carry special articles by the experts on certain phases of the game. *Golf World* is a weekly golf magazine that occasionally offers instruction along with a continuing report of the American and even international golf world, both professional and amateur. You may find considerable enjoyment in picking one of the newest members of the professional tour and following his career, tournament by tournament.

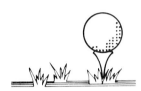

chapter 39

A GLOSSARY OF TERMS

Better Ball—The better score between a pair of golfers on the same hole. Example: A and B, partners, have 4 and 5, respectively. The better ball of the pair is 4. In club competitions, sometimes the two better balls, or even the best three of a foursome, are used to register a score. For Example, A has a 4, B a 5, C a 6, and D a 7 in a foursome in club competition. The two better balls of the foursome would be the 4 and 5 for a score of 9 on the hole. The three best balls would be the 4, 5, and 6 for a score of 15. The best ball of the foursome would be the 4, of course.

Birdie—A score of 1 under par for a hole, e.g., a 2 on a 3-par hole, a 3 on a 4-par hole, a 4 on a 5-par hole.

Bogey—A score of 1 over par for a hole, e.g., a 4 on a 3-par, a 5 on a 4-par, a 6 on a 5-par.

Closed Stance—One in which the right foot is placed to the right of the line toward the target, farther away from that line than the left foot, while the left foot remains square to that line. This stance is conducive to a hook.

Dormie—In match play the reckoning of holes is kept by the terms: so many "holes up" or "all square" and so many "to play." A side is a "dormie" when it is as many holes up as there are holes remaining to be played. A good term to know and use correctly.

Double Bogey—A score of 2 over par for a hole.

Double Eagle—The term applied to the rare feat of holing out in 2 strokes on a 5-par hole or scoring an ace on a 4-par hole.

Down—Expression used in match play to denote the state of the match for the losing player. Example:

```
A:    5   4   3   5
B:    6   7   4   6
```

B is 4 holes down to A through the fourth hole. The match ends when either golfer is ahead by more holes than there are holes left to play. Example with A and B even at the tenth hole of a match:

second A:	3 4 3 4 4 4 5 5 6	B wins 1 up
9 holes: B:	3 4 3 4 4 4 5 5 5	
second A:	3 4 3 4 4 4	A wins 3 up with 2
9 holes: B:	3 4 3 5 5 5 4	holes to play
second A:	3 4 3 4 4 4	A wins 4 up with 2
9 holes: B:	3 4 3 5 5 5 5	holes to play

Half—A "half" occurs when golfers tie a hole in the same score. When handicaps are in effect, it is the net score that is "halved."

Hook—A ball that curves from right to left in the air as a result of counterclockwise spin imparted by the face of the golf club at impact.

Nassau Bet—A system of betting based upon match play with 3 points at stake, 1 point on each nine holes, independently, and 1 on the total eighteen-hole match. When the players tie, the points are split. Examples of results: A wins 2½ to B's ½ or A and B tie the match with each player getting 1½ points.

Open Stance—One in which the left foot of the golfer is placed to the left of the line toward the target, farther away from that line than the right foot, while the right foot remains square to that line. This stance is conducive to a slice.

Par—The established score that an expert golfer would be expected to make for a given hole. Par means errorless play under ordinary weather conditions, allowing 2 strokes on the putting green. Ordinarily, the par of a hole is determined by its length. Here are the pars and yardages for men and women players as suggested by the United States Golf Association:

	Men	Women
Par 3	up to 250 yards	up to 210 yards
Par 4	251 to 470	211 to 400
Par 5	471 and over	401 to 575
Par 6		576 and over

Press—The name given to an extra bet entered into by the golfers along the way as one opponent or the other becomes "down" to the other, usually by at least two holes. Sometimes a press bet is "automatic," meaning it goes into effect when the conditions occur; at other times it must be negotiated by the golfer who is "down."

Pull—A shot that goes straight, but on a line to the left of that intended by the golfer.

Push—A shot that goes straight but on a line to the right of that intended by the golfer.

Sclaff—A wonderful old expression meaning to hit the ground behind the golf ball first, striking the ball as the swing continues.

Slice—A ball that curves from left to right in the air as a result of clockwise spin imparted by the face of the golf club at impact.

Up—The golfer who is ahead in match play is said to be "up" on the other by the number of holes he has won. Example:

A:	4	5	5	8	7	A is 1 up on B at the
B:	5	6	7	6	6	end of 5 holes

index

O

Obstructions, relief from, 121
"One number stronger theory," 95, 96
"One-piece" takeaway, 31
One-third swing, 65
"Opening the face," 149
Out-of-bounds, 120, 121
Overlapping, 12, 13

P

Palmer, Arnold, 49
"Pencil bag," 129
Percentage of perfection, 114
Picking up the club, 32
Pitch shot, 95
Player, Gary, 7, 79, 99
Plum Hollow Golf Club, 25
Practice, 111, 140
Professional Golfers Association, 28, 133, 157
Professional Golfers Tour, 7
Provisional ball, 120, 122
Putting games, 86, 87
Putting green, 122
Putting strokes, 73
    All-arm method, 73, 74
    Arm-wrist method, 73, 74

Q

Quinn, James, 117

R

Rain, 137
Rainstorm, 135
Release through the ball, 57
Right side of the cup, 83
Romack, Barbara, 9
Rosburg, Bob, 13
Ross, Alex, 5
Rhythm and balance, 43
Royal and Ancient Golf Club, 119
Rules of Golf, 119, 123

S

Safety, 163
Sand shot, 99
Sanders, Doug, 49
Scorecard, keeping a, 169–171
Semi-private, 165
Semi-public, 165
"Shank zone," 163

Sidehill lie, 152
Smith, Horton, 5, 39, 43, 54, 74, 75, 84, 85
Snead, Sam, 157
Spalding, 130
Spike marks, 122
Sponsor, 167
Stance, 121
St. Andrews, 119, 155
Sarazen, Gene, 99
Shell Oil Company, 116
Short thumb, 14, 15
Shoulder tilt, 22
Special situations, 149
Stances, 35
Standard clubs, 133
Standing tall, 59
Start-down, 53
Staying down to the ball, 147
Steady head, 27
Stop at the top, 49
Straight left arm, 39
Stranahan, Frank, 7
Strategy, 103
Strategy of the tee shot, 107–109
Squareness to the line, 83
Strong position, 16
Superstitions of golf, 127, 128
Sweeping, 87
"Sweet spot," 87, 88
Swing faults, 159
Swing plane, 20
Swing-weight, 133

T

Takeaway, 45, 140
Target, 112
Taylor, J. H., 12, 173
Tee, 107
Teeing area, 107, 108
Tee-markets, 107, 120
Tee-shot, 109
Tension, 47, 49
Three-quarter position, 49
Top of the backswing, 47
Trevino, Lee, 49
Trouble, 145
Two-thirds swing, 65, 67, 68
Twisting devices, 140

U

Umbrella, 135
Uneven lies, 150